To: Hon. Sherr Eisenpress

A HISTORY OF DIVORCE

By

S. B. KITCHIN, B.A., LL.B.

*Late Scholar of Trinity Hall, Cambridge; Advocate of the Supreme
Court of South Africa; Member of the Provincial
Council of the Cape of Good Hope; Editor
of the Reports of the High Court
of Griqualand, 1905-10.*

LONDON:

CHAPMAN & HALL, Ltd.

1912

PREFACE

SO far as I am aware, there is no book in the English language which gives a concise and simple account of the history of divorce, and there is no modern problem in which the historical and comparative study of law and opinion is so essential for those who administer or make the laws, and all those who wish to have an adequate knowledge of the subject in its modern bearings. The extraordinary diversity of laws and opinions which exists in modern countries of the same degree of civilisation, often professing the same religion, when seen in the light of history is found to have certain common elements which show that substantially the same forces have been at work in their evolution. The object of this book is to explain, as briefly and simply as I can, how this diversity came about, to endeavour to deduce from the facts of history the tendencies of thought and legislation, and to ascertain the principles which, according to the teaching of history, ought to be applied to modern legislation on the subject.

PREFACE

"It is mostly in periods of turmoil, strife and confusion," says William Morris, "that people care much about history," and it cannot be denied that the present is a time of unrest and dissatisfaction with many institutions dating from bygone days which profoundly affect the welfare of mankind.

"History of this undefined and international cast, which shows the same wave beating upon many shores, is difficult," as the late Lord Acton said, but the fact that the wave is the same in substance, though different in form and volume in different generations and countries, renders the difficulty not insuperable. It will be found that that wave, as applied to the history of divorce, is composed of almost equal parts of liberty on the one hand and dogma on the other, as represented by the principles of the Roman and the Ecclesiastical or Canon laws respectively. In other words, the history of divorce is not the least important, and is certainly one of the most typical chapters of the "History of Freedom," and its land-marks are those of that history.

It need hardly be said that this book does not claim to be a complete history of the subject, especially as it has been written, for the most part, thousands of miles away from

PREFACE

the great libraries and historical repositories
of Europe. Such a history, covering the period
of this book, the whole of civilisation from the
beginning of Christianity to our own time, would
have required not twelve short chapters, but as
many long volumes, and, according to modern
methods, at least as many persons to write it.
The maxim of Erasmus—" Read first the
best books on the subject which you have
in hand "—may, however, be borne in mind.
I have therefore sought for principles and
tendencies rather than a mass of detail, and
the reader who is more fortunately placed will
be able to obtain additional illustrations and
details from his own reading. It has been my
aim to seek the original sources in the texts of the
laws themselves, which reflect the aspirations of
those who made them and the state of mind of
those who were expected to obey them, and in
the leading authorities of the different centuries
and countries under review. I have also tried
to show how the various intellectual, moral
and religious movements affected law and opinion
on the subject, and for this purpose I have made
full use of the most authoritative general histories.
A book like the present, which deals with what
Lord Acton aptly called " the remunerative but
perilous region where religion and politics con-

flict," could not have been written without estimating, and in some measure criticising, the operation of the various religious beliefs on the theory and practice of divorce. Such beliefs have been treated throughout, not on their theological merits, but solely as historical forces, and wherever dogma has been made into law it has been treated as law.

The principles of legislation which are enunciated in this book appear to me to be clearly deducible from the authorities which have been accessible to me, and I have as far as possible allowed those authorities—many of them for the first time—to speak for themselves in the plain and simple language of our own day. This little book will, it is hoped, serve as an introduction to those who wish to study the subject in greater detail or in relation to any particular country, and it will not have been written in vain if it is the means of encouraging a spirit of greater sympathy and tolerance towards those—especially women, who have had little or no voice in the making of the laws—who are, often through no fault of their own, made to suffer for the well-meant but often misguided laws and opinions of our ancestors.

I should like to take this opportunity of thanking all those who have been kind enough

PREFACE

to place their libraries at my disposal, and especially to express my acknowledgments to the various living authorities whose works have been cited in the course of this work : in particular to the editors and authors of *The Journal of the Society of Comparative Legislation, The Law Quarterly Review,* Burge's *Commentaries on Colonial and Foreign Laws,* and *The Cambridge Modern History.* I am also indebted to Mr. Leal, of the Lourenço Marques Bar, for a translation of the new divorce law of the Portuguese Republic ; and, finally, to my friend, Mr. R. W. Lee, Professor of Roman-Dutch Law at the University College, London, for his kindness in correcting the proofs for me, and for his assistance in seeing the book through the press.

S. B. KITCHIN.

Cape Town,
    March, 1912.

CONTENTS

CONTENTS

CONTENTS

CONTENTS

CONTENTS

CONTENTS

ROMAN DIVORCE

I

ROMAN DIVORCE

"If marriages are made by mutual affection, it is only right that when that affection no longer exists they should be dissoluble by mutual consent."—JUSTIN, Novel 140.

"THE Romans," says Mr. Bryce, "built up the marriage laws of the civilised world." The principle which has been given at the head of this chapter in the words of one of the Christian Emperors was, like Rome, "not built in a day," but was only established after a long struggle on the part of married women to obtain equal rights in marriage and divorce. In the early days of Rome, as in most early communities, the wife was looked upon as the property of her husband, who either bought her, or acquired her by prescription or by a religious ceremony. Afterwards she came to be regarded not as his property but as his child. As he had the power of life and death over her, the law stepped in at an early date and provided that instead of killing her when he was tired of her, or whenever she asserted her independence— which he was now only allowed to do if she were taken in adultery—he might divorce her, and, as

1

a further protection for the wife, laid down that unless she were guilty of " perverse morals " he had to provide for her maintenance after divorce. Whenever she was guilty she had to forfeit a portion of her dowry to her husband as a sort of consolation for him. The wife had never any right to the children, who became her husband's as soon as they were born. Divorce, therefore, though invented for the protection of women, was for a long time the sole prerogative of men, who made the laws and called the woman's conduct perverse just as it suited them. The earliest known case of divorce in Rome is that of a patrician who divorced his wife, not on account of her conduct, but because she was unable to bear him children. The reason why the poets thought fit to hand it down to posterity was that popular indignation had been aroused by the interference of the censors, whose duty it was, not only to protect public morals, but also to see that the list of citizens was well filled. They had made the husband take an oath that he would divorce her because she was barren, in order that he might marry again and provide children for the State. The first known case of Roman divorce was therefore said to have been in the interests of public policy. This, however, was not the first case of divorce, for the early

2

laws provided that the husband might divorce his wife if she were guilty of drinking wine, of going out without a veil, speaking to a woman of inferior rank in the street, or going to a place of public amusement without her husband's consent; all these being regarded as perversity of morals. In all these cases the husband incurred no penalty or moral blame for the divorce, and he was relieved of the necessity of maintaining his wife after divorce.*

Divorce in early Rome was practically the same as it was among the Jews at the time of Christ. It was said by the old Hebrew authorities to have been permitted for the sake of domestic peace, to check the pride or disobedience of wives and the anger of husbands. No public trial was necessary in either system, the only formality being the delivery to the wife of a bill of divorce. Moses appears to have introduced this formality, and to have attempted to define certain grounds for divorce for the protection of women. The right of divorce by women was, however, not unknown among the Jews, although the woman had to go to court whenever she required divorce, and when the court decided that she was entitled to it, the

* Brouwer II, 31 ; Montesquieu XVI, 16 ; Heineccius, *Antiquitatum Romanarum Syntagma*, Appendix, Book I, § 45 ; Muirhead, *History of the Roman Law*, 2nd ed., ch. iii and foll.

husband was bound to give her a bill of divorce. It is clear, however, that whatever provision Moses and the Rabbis made for divorce was intended to protect woman from injustice where she did not consent to the divorce; and though divorce by the wife was in some cases recognised, the Hebrew wife did not obtain an equal right of divorce till the eleventh century A.D. The interpretation of disobedience to the husband as " perverse morals " and as a ground for divorce has Biblical authority, for we are told that Ahasuerus divorced Vashti because she refused to obey his command to appear before him at a feast and display her beauty to the princes assembled, when he was " merry with wine "; the divorce was, as the Bible states, intended as a perpetual lesson to wives who ventured to disobey their husbands. " If thy wife go not as thou wouldst have her," says Jesus, the son of Sirach, " give her a bill of divorce and let her go." This effective difference between the rights of husband and wife was the result of the wife being regarded as " anything that is his," and when the wife became capable of owning property of her own, and acquired an independent legal personality, she became capable also of consenting to a divorce, of exercising an equal right of divorce, and of having an equal right to the children born of the marriage.*

By the time of Christ Roman marriage had become a private partnership of the most intimate nature, in which the parties were equal, and shared in all rights. As marriage was founded on affection and consent, the parties had the right to dissolve it, when that affection had turned into aversion, either by consent or by one of them giving formal notice to the other, exactly like any other partnership, and no judicial or other inquiry into the causes of the divorce was necessary. So far from divorce being regarded as dishonourable, all agreements between the parties forbidding the right of divorce were held to be void and an infringement of the rule that " marriages ought to be free." To compel an unwilling party to remain married was as unthinkable to the Romans as to compel an unwilling party to enter into marriage. As Mr. Bryce says : "Compulsion in any form is utterly opposed to a connection which springs from free choice and is sustained by affection only." No public ceremony was necessary, marriage being formed by the intention of

* Pufendorf II, vi, 1, 23 and foll.; Brouwer II, 23 ; Deut. xxiv, 1-4 ; Esther I ; Ecclesiasticus XXV, 26 ; Selden, *Uxor Ebraica*, 3, 22-26 ; Jewish Encyclopædia, *s.v.* divorce ; Abrahams, *Jewish Life in the Middle Ages*, pp. 80-90, 121, 175-6.

the parties, of which the best evidence was living together as man and wife. "Marriage cannot be said to exist," says Ulpian, "where the parties are separated." This constitution of marriage without any public ceremony, except 'certain customary or " decorative " ceremonies, remained the practice of Europe until the Reformation in the sixteenth century, when for the first time the necessity of a public ceremony was laid down. The informal marriage of the Roman law still survives and is recognised as binding in Scotland. *

Divorce, like marriage, was in the Roman law purely a private matter between the parties, depending upon their intention. It was only necessary that it should be formal and final, the ceremony of divorce being similar to that when a last will was made. The one spouse delivered to the other, through a messenger and in the presence of seven witnesses, a letter expressing the intention to put an end to the marriage, and saying that the other might in future keep his or her own property, but no ground for divorce was stated. If the letter of divorce was delivered in sudden anger, it was not binding until it had been ratified by a

* Brouwer II, 31 ; Dig. xxiv, 2 ; Cod. 5, 17 ; Bryce II, xvi ; Burge, 2nd ed., III, p. 190.

6

final determination; if after the delivery the divorcing party changed his mind, the other could become the divorcing party. The divorce might be either by consent or " with a good grace " (*bona gratia*), as it was called, or as one may say *dulciter in modo sed fortiter in re*, or it might be against the wish of one of them (*mala gratia*).*

A judicial inquiry into the causes of the divorce was only necessary when the parties could not come to terms about the future of the children and the division of the property. As they were not obliged to publicly prosecute each other before obtaining a divorce, they would agree in most cases about these matters, and separate amicably, without that bitter animosity which the modern public trial always leaves behind it. In the rare cases where they could not settle the terms of the dissolution of the partnership, the court, at the request of either party, settled these matters after divorce, as in any other partnership dispute. The basis of judicial settlement in such cases depended upon the question of moral blame attaching to one or other of the parties, and the old rule of the forfeiture of a

* Brouwer, *ubi supra;* Moyle, *Institutes of Justinian,* Book I, tit. 10 ; Cod. 8, 9, 32 ; Dig. xxiv, 2 ; Pothier ad Pandectas xxiv, 2.

certain amount of property in the other's favour by the one who had been guilty of " perverse morals " remained, wherever the innocent party sought such forfeiture. This action was for this reason called a " moral action," though this name afterwards disappeared, and it became under Justinian an ordinary action of contract. So repugnant, however, to the Romans was any public inquiry into the secrets of family life that for a long time these matters were settled by a family council; this was turned later into a public inquiry before a judge, probably because where the spouses were unable to agree about these matters the relatives would be no less unlikely to come to an agreement. The judge in this way obtained a discretion as to the care and custody of the children, which he used in their interest, though the question of morality largely influenced his decision. After divorce each party had to contribute towards the education and maintenance of the children, according to their means. If the parties were equally guilty of " perverse morals," or if the husband had connived at his wife's adultery for the purposes of gain, the judge refused to interfere, and left the parties in possession of whatever property each possessed.*

* Dig. xxiv, 2 & 3, and Pothier thereon; Muirhead's *History of the Roman Law*, 2nd ed., p. 234.

ROMAN DIVORCE

As divorce was a private matter between the parties and not a legal action at all, the rule that the domicil of the wife followed that of her husband did not apply, and the wife was not obliged to follow her husband wherever he went. If for any reason the one could not give notice of the divorce to the other, the divorce was not invalidated. If one of them had been absent for a long time without news or was in exile or captivity, this did not prevent divorce, and where it took place no moral blame attached to either party. Similarly, where one of the spouses was suffering from some serious disease, such as insanity, divorce was still possible if the other party wished for it. The Romans in such cases simply considered whether either was morally to blame, and if the disease was intolerable or incurable, there was no blame in either of them. The Roman maxim that nothing was more humane than that each spouse should bear the accidental misfortunes of the other was never applied as a legal rule by the Romans to prevent divorce altogether, if the healthy spouse did not choose to share in such misfortunes; if indeed the sharing of such misfortunes, where one of them is confined for life in a lunatic asylum, is possible, or the insane spouse can be said to suffer by the other party marrying again. In all these misfortunes the Romans held that marriage depended on the affection of the parties, and when that affection had ceased either party had the right to dissolve the marriage.*

Such were the main principles of Roman divorce which have remained in force in some form or other in various parts of Europe. Their vitality, whether as actual living law or as a legislative force which has from time to time asserted itself in history, is due to the fact that they were based upon liberty and equality, and upon the wishes and welfare of the people. The Roman legislators always recognised that it made no difference whether the people declared their wishes by their votes or by their customs. "These principles," says Mr. Bryce, "have a special interest as being the last word of ancient civilisation before Christianity began to influence legislation. They have in them much that is elevated, much that is attractive. They embody the doctrines which, after an interval of many centuries, have again begun to be preached with the fervour of conviction to the modern world, especially in England and the United States, by many zealous friends of progress,

* Pothier, *ubi supra* ; Cod. 5, 17, 6.

10

and especially by those who think that the greatest step towards progress is to be found in what is called the emancipation of women."*

An inquiry into the practice of these principles by the Roman people need not detain us long, because the evidence is very meagre, and, such as it is, is generally of a partisan nature. The laws themselves, which remained in practice for centuries in the most practical nation of antiquity, which were built upon the purity and integrity of family life, are probably sufficient in themselves to show their utility. The opinion, however, has frequently been asserted that divorce was frequent among the Romans, and it has been strongly contended that the Roman law of divorce was the efficient, if not the sole, cause of immorality. The evidence which we have refers mainly to a short period about the end of the Republic and the beginning of the Empire, and consists of a few isolated statements by comic poets and Fathers of the Church, notably Tertullian and Jerome. Gibbon, who in a famous rhetorical passage relies solely upon the same evidence, has taken the opportunity of making a somewhat hasty generalisation. "A specious theory," he says, "is confuted by this free and perfect experi-

* Bryce, *ubi supra.*

11

ment, which demonstrates that the liberty of
divorce does not contribute to happiness and
virtue." Although Gibbon could not be said
to have any ecclesiastical bias in the matter, he
certainly had the strong bias against the rights
of women which prevailed in the eighteenth
century, and most of the denunciations of
Roman divorce have emanated from those
who, like Gibbon, make a distinction between
adultery when it is committed by husband and
wife respectively, always excusing the former
and condemning the latter. Impartial modern
authorities, however, such as the late Mr. Lecky
and Mr. L. T. Hobhouse, have pointed out that
the evidence upon which these denunciations are
based is meagre, exaggerated and unreliable.
It is noteworthy that Gibbon himself says of the
statements on which he relies that they are "an
extravagant hyperbole," while that of Jerome
is as much a condemnation of second marriages
after the death of the first spouse as of divorces.
The views of the early Fathers of the Church on
divorce and second and later marriages will be
examined in the next chapter. The conduct of
a few wealthy men and women during the few
years to which this evidence refers, in Rome,
out of a population of something over a hundred
and twenty millions in the whole Empire, where

the same law remained in force until at least the tenth century, can scarcely be regarded as typical. The question of the connection between divorce and morality is at most speculative. Rome was just as immoral and was the same " sewer of the nations " at that time as it was when Luther visited it in the sixteenth century, when marriage was indissoluble. A useful parallel might be drawn between Rome at the beginning of the Empire, and England at the time of the Restoration, when marriage was well-nigh indissoluble, and, as Dryden says, polygamy was no sin. As Mr. Lecky says of the Romans : " Of those who scandalised good men by the rapid recurrence of their marriages, probably most, if marriage had been indissoluble, would have refrained from entering into it, and would have contented themselves with many informal connections, or if they had married, would have gratified their love of change by simple adultery. A vast wave of corruption had flowed in upon Rome, and under any system of law it would have penetrated into domestic life." Both Mr. Lecky and Mr. Hobhouse also point out that that time also contained " most of those noble examples of the constancy of Roman wives, which have been for so many generations household tales among mankind."

A HISTORY OF DIVORCE

The condemnation of Roman divorce has always emanated principally from those who in some form or other have advocated the dogma of the indissolubility of marriage, or have followed the long tradition of associating divorce solely with some crime or immoral act. The utility of the Roman law and the alleged connection between divorce and immorality will be better appreciated and estimated when the later history of divorce in Europe has been examined.*

---

* Lecky, *History of European Morals*, II, v, pp. 306 and foll. ; L. T. Hobhouse, *Morals in Evolution*, I, pp. 215 and foll. ; Gibbon, *Decline and Fall of the Roman Empire* (Methuen's Standard Library), vol. IV, ch. xliv, pp. 479 and foll., and p. 503, note 195 ; Muirhead's *History of the Roman Law*, 2nd ed., p. 356 ; Dryden, *Absolom and Achitophel* (opening lines).

THE FATHERS OF THE
EARLY CHURCH

c

II

THE FATHERS OF THE EARLY CHURCH

"All these matters, which some will deem superfluous, and others heretical, we have handled with great fear and caution, discussing and debating rather than affirming and defining . . . . . . God alone knows how things will be."

ORIGEN (cited in Bigg's "Origins of Christianity," p. 442.)

THE views of the early Fathers and the practice of the Early Christian Church have had a great influence upon the law of divorce. Apologists of the doctrine of the indissolubility of marriage, as well as those who have regarded marriage as dissoluble on certain Scriptural grounds, have always regarded the practice of the Church, or of some portion of it, during the first few centuries of its existence—some relying upon the first six and some upon the first three centuries—as being conclusive of the matter. Such apologists, however, appear to be in the same unfortunate position as Abraham, who vainly endeavoured to save Sodom from destruction by pleading that it contained a gradually-diminishing number of righteous men. The fact is that not one century nor one year can be found in the history of the

17

Church or of Europe when the indissolubility of marriage was ever practised, and the history of the Early Church is characterised by the same want of unity of interpretation as has been found among all who have endeavoured to make their interpretations of the well-known Scriptural texts the basis of the law of divorce.[1] As Mr. Hobhouse says: " The deliverances of the New Testament being uncertain, the views of the early Fathers waver, just as the views of the Canonists and Reformers diametrically differ." *

The bishops from apostolic times exercised jurisdiction over their flocks in obedience to the Scriptural command that the faithful should abstain from litigation. So litigious did this jurisdiction become that the Christian Emperors had to check the bishops in its exercise, because it interfered with their spiritual functions. There is no evidence, however, that the bishops of the Early Church exercised jurisdiction over divorce, which was always treated in law as a private matter, and the Church appears to have interfered only when after divorce the question arose whether either of the parties should be allowed the blessing of the Church upon entering into a second marriage. According to the

* L. T. Hobhouse, *Morals in Evolution*, I, p. 218.

canons of the Church of St. Clement of Rome, if a layman divorced his wife and married again, or if anyone married a divorced woman, he might be excommunicated and was incapacitated from becoming a priest. But these very canons show that the right of divorce and re-marriage was not interfered with by the Church. The Roman law was observed in all parts of the Empire, and the Church by its councils, and the Fathers by their opinions, never appear to have disputed it in any way, and they were indeed responsible for the insertion of many of its provisions in Imperial legislation. The Church from time to time endeavoured to lay down that the cause of divorce must have its approval in all cases, and at a council in the year 416, at which St. Augustine assisted, it was proposed to abolish divorce altogether and to try to obtain Imperial legislation to that effect, the parties being condemned to remain celibate or become reconciled. Such legislation, however, never was obtained, until Charlemagne at the beginning of the ninth century inserted this resolution in his Capitularies.*

The Fathers of the Church did not pretend to have any more inspiration upon the subject of

---

* Muirhead, p. 357 ; *Canones Apostolorum*, §§ 17 & 47 (circa 300 A.D.) ; Groenewegen ad Cod., 5, 17 ; Pothier, *Mariage*, § 492 ; Brouwer II, ch. 31.

divorce than St. Paul, whose views greatly
influenced them, and who allowed divorce where
one party did not choose to live with the other
owing to certain religious differences. They
interpreted the texts of the Scriptures as written
laws which were binding upon the consciences
of all Christians; but, although some of them
were lawyers, they do not appear to have
observed the ordinary rule of interpretation
that where conflicting laws restrict the liberty
of the subject the interpretation the most favourable to human liberty must be followed, and,
above all, that regard must be had to the rule
volenti non fit injuria. Marriage was by all of
them regarded as an inferior condition to that
of celibacy. Their guiding principle was the
well-known text, " It is better to marry than to
burn." ' Few texts," as Pollock and Maitland
say, "have done more harm than this. . . .
The law that springs from this source is not
pleasant reading." Marriage being regarded as
a " defilement " or " truly fornication," as it
was variously expressed, a second marriage,
whether after divorce or after the death of one
of the parties, was " a species of adultery," for
as the Church had " one God for a husband," so
marriage, if entered into at all by those who
were weak enough to indulge in it, should never

20

be made use of again. Jerome execrated a woman who married again after the death of her husband, calling her " a dog returning to its vomit and a washed sow returning to its wallowing-place." The inordinate influence of the sexual passions and a reaction in favour of celibacy, which impelled Origen to mutilate himself and St. Augustine to bewail his marriage as much as his earlier experiences of concubinage, must be taken into account in estimating the views which the Fathers held upon divorce and upon women. Their views on women were taken from the teaching of St. Paul and from North Africa and the East, where most of them originated. Marriage as a refuge from fornication or a matter of convenience, and woman as a source of sin, and indeed the source of original sin, which the Fathers insist upon, could have no meaning to the Romans. A married woman was expected by St. Augustine to look upon her marriage-lines as " indentures of perpetual service," and to " joyfully endure the debaucheries and ill-treatment of her lord." Where marriage, once entered into, was regarded as a sacrament which only crime could dissolve, and its outward observance was inculcated at all costs, especially for women, the countenancing of polygamy and prostitution by St.

21

Augustine followed almost logically from his views on marriage. A prostitute was in his view as necessary to a city as a sewer was to a palace, and polygamy he could not condemn, as the Bible has not forbidden it. It is clear that the world in which the Fathers moved, and the Eastern notions with which they were imbued, can have no application to modern life, where few would venture to advocate such a low view of marriage or of woman in the name of Christianity. Marriage was regarded as a sort of mutual prison from which there was no escape except by the commission of a crime. Marriage being a confession of weakness, divorce was a confession of greater weakness. The human affections were regarded as of no account, and submission to whatever political or civil condition men and women found themselves in was the essence of patristic teaching. To regard the tenets of the Fathers as binding upon modern life would be as valuable as to accept the views of those who objected to all prisons and yet said that once people were in prison they must remain there all their lives, and joyfully endure as the will of God whatever punishment the most inhuman gaoler might inflict upon them.*

* St. Paul, 1 Cor. vii, 9 & 15 & *passim* ; Grat. Decret. xxxii, 4-7 ; Pollock and Maitland, II, p. 383 ; Lecky, *History of European Morals*, II, ch. v; Leyser spec., 300; Rittershusius II, 1 ; Leo, Novel 90 ; St. Augus-

FATHERS OF THE EARLY CHURCH

The theories of the Fathers upon the subject of divorce are as uncertain and as conflicting as the well-known texts upon which they are based. Though they did not, as we have seen, purport to make laws, the expression of their views has always been regarded as a source of law by all who have attempted to base human law upon the shifting sands of Scriptural interpretations. [While none of them doubted that "fornication" was the principal ground for divorce, according to those texts, they differed considerably as to what that word meant, interpreting it to mean variously—adultery, suspicion of adultery, spiritual adultery, heresy, blasphemy, unlawful desires or worldly views, or some other criminal or immoral act; while some of them doubted whether the Church should extend its blessing to one or both of the parties upon a second marriage, and some again made a distinction between the rights of husband and of wife.* F6

[Justin Martyr, the earliest of the Fathers, in an address to the Roman Senate, commended a Christian wife, who, taking advantage of the

tine, *Confessions* & *De Civitate Dei*, Lib., xiii; Brouwer I, xxvii, 15; Grotius, *Rights of Peace and War*, II, v, 9—note by Barbeyrac ; Groen. ad Cod. v, 10 *pr.*

* Matth. v. 27-32 & xix, 1-12 ; Mark x, 1-12 ; Luke xvi, 18 ; 1 Cor. vii, 15 ; Matth. xix, 11 & xxii, 23-30 ; Mark xii, 18-25 & John *passim* ; Esp. iv, 16-19 & viii, 3 ; Luke vi, 36-50 ; Deut. xxiv, 1-4 & xxi, 15.

Roman law, divorced her husband because of his debaucheries, so that she might not partake of his crimes by living with him. In the third century, Tertullian, who practised for some time at the bar in Rome, held that adultery was a ground for divorce according to the Divine law. Origen regarded adultery as only one example of offences which justified divorce. The bishops had given their blessing to the re-marriage of a woman who had divorced her husband because of his immoral conduct, and Origen approved of this, although he considered that she was technically an adulteress for marrying again. The bishops and the eminent Father, however, were prepared to waive a technicality of that kind. Chrysostom, in the fourth century, said that divorce was permitted by the Divine law because it was better that a marriage should be dissolved than that the parties should, by being compelled to live together, when they hated each other, be induced to commit murder. Basil allowed divorce on the ground of adultery, but said that Christ only spoke of the right of the husband, and that it was an ancient custom of the Church that the same right did not apply to the wife. Jerome said that whenever there was adultery or suspicion of adultery, the wife might be divorced without scruple. He, however, did not allow the same right to the wife. His famous words, " So long as the husband lives, whether he be an adulterer or a sodomist, or be steeped in all manner of crime and the wife has left him on account of those crimes, he is still to be regarded as her husband, and she is not allowed to marry again," express the nadir of the matrimonial degradation of women, and afterwards became the basis of the treatment of women under the Canon law. It may be remembered that Luther said of Jerome that " he teaches nothing about faith, or hope, or love." Epiphanius allowed divorce on the ground of adultery or other crime, and said that, if either party married again, the Church absolved them from all blame, tolerated their weakness, and did not reject them either from the Church or from eternal life.*

St. Augustine has generally been regarded as the pillar of the indissolubility of marriage, and his utterances have been looked upon as oracles. His views are characteristic of all oracles, and of all attempts to base the law of

* Grotius, *De jure belli ac pacis*, 2, 5, 9, and Barbeyrac's Notes; Groen. ad Cod., 5, 17; Gratian Decret., 32, 7, 7; Pothier, *Mariage*, §§ 487 and foll. ; Gore, *The Question of Divorce*, pp. 34-5 ; *Encyclopædia Britannica*, 11th ed., as to the biographies of the various Fathers; Rittershusius 2, 1.

divorce upon the Scriptural texts. He admits the right of the husband and therefore of the wife, according to the Scriptures, to a divorce on the ground of adultery, but he says of the text which states that if they marry again they commit adultery, that it is so obscure and difficult that any one is justified in making a mistake in the matter.(*ut, quantum existimo, venialiter ibi quisque fallatur*). He says that after writing two books upon marriage and divorce according to the Scriptures, he dare not flatter himself that he has succeeded in clearing up the very difficult and knotty questions involved. He rather feels that he has not arrived at perfect truth in the matter, although he hopes that he has made a good many openings which the intelligent reader may judge of and make use of for himself. We have seen how, in order to settle a subtle question which this most subtle of Fathers was unable to disentangle, he finally decided to cut the Gordian knot by declaring the absolute indissolubility of marriage.*

Lord Lyndhurst, during the debate on the English Divorce Bill in 1857, cleared away any doubts which may have remained as to the authority of St. Augustine in this matter. Having examined the voluminous writings of

* Pothier, *Marriage*, §§ 487, 491-2.

26

St. Augustine, the ex-Lord Chancellor said that he had been struck with the singular subtlety of that high authority in drawing fine distinctions, and that " that distinguished divine was more skilful in creating difficulties than in discovering methods of removing them." He had laid down repeatedly that adultery was an undoubted ground for divorce for either husband or wife, although he could not make up his mind as to the exact meaning of adultery, and whether it might not be extended to include " any unlawful desires or worldly views." Lord Lyndhurst told an anecdote illustrating the doubts of the learned Father. A man had been thrown into prison at Antioch for not paying his taxes, and had been threatened with the penalty of death unless he paid them. His wife, who was very handsome, was approached by a wealthy man, who offered to redeem her husband on condition that she should spend the night with him. After some hesitation she consulted her husband, who, like the weak brother in *Measure for Measure*, advised her to accept the offer, which she did. The question was afterwards submitted to St. Augustine as to whether this was adultery or not. After referring to the texts which said that the spouses had certain rights over each other's bodies, he found himself unable to give

27

a decision, and said that he would leave every one to form his own judgment ; " which," said Lord Lyndhurst, " showed his caution." St. Augustine not only doubted whether divorce should be allowed for any other cause than adultery, but he even " had great doubts whether the parties should be allowed to marry again." " I do not find," concluded Lord Lyndhurst, " that he came to any decisive conclusion. So much for the authority of St. Augustine." And so much for the authority of the Fathers of the Church.*

* Hansard, vol. 146, pp. 1689 and foll.

III

THE CHRISTIAN EMPERORS OF ROME

"It is said that by marriage the two become one flesh
and that each member ought to suffer all the diseases of
the other, and the divine precept is that those whom God
has joined should not be separated. These are excellent
and indeed divine words, seeing that they were pronounced
by God himself. But they are not in point here, nor are
they cited in accordance with the intention of their divine
author. For if marriage always remained in the same condition as it was when it began, whoever separated himself
from it would indeed be wicked and would not escape
censure."—LEO, Novel 111.

THE influence of the Church upon divorce
legislation begins with Constantine,
who, at the beginning of the fourth
century, inaugurated the alliance between
Church and State. The Christian Emperors
who promulgated their laws "in the name of
our Lord Jesus Christ" regarded themselves as
the protectors of the Church, at whose councils
they often presided, and of its dogma, much of
which they defined and made into secular laws.
Justinian says in the Code that he follows the
dogma of the Church, and accordingly defines
its creed, and, "desiring to imitate the con-

31   D

descension of Christ," anathematises all heretics. The Emperors began interfering in the law of divorce by applying the prevailing ecclesiastical opinions to it, restricting the rights of the wife and laying down certain grounds for divorce, generally crimes, the only grounds upon which spouses might divorce each other without incurring any penalty. Divorce, however, was always allowed to remain a private matter between the parties, and divorce by mutual consent, which they did not consider to be contrary to the Scriptures, was not interfered with. Divorce for any other cause was punished by the infliction of certain penalties, such as the forfeiture of a certain amount of property to the other spouse or to the Church or State, and in some cases by banishment or condemnation to celibacy for a certain period. Similar penalties were as a rule inflicted upon the guilty party, who had by the commission of one of the specified crimes given the innocent party the right to a divorce.[*]

Without going through the long story of the gradual evolution of pains and penalties for unlawful divorce, due to fluctuating interpretations of the Scriptures, the result of this legislation may be summarised by a reference to the Code of the "royal dogmatist," Justinian.

[*] Cod. 1, 1-16 and 5, 17; Brouwer II, ch. xxxi.

The grounds upon which a wife might divorce
her husband without blame or penalty were,
firstly, the adultery of the husband with a
married woman " in contempt of the home "
(*i.e.*, in their own house or in the same town after
frequent warnings). Such an offence, when so
committed, was said by one of the Emperors to
be " the cause of the greatest exasperation to
chaste women." Other grounds were the
commission by the husband of certain crimes,
such as murder, fraud, sacrilege or treason.
Cruelty to a wife had been impossible where
under the old Roman law the wife had the right
of divorce, and some of the Emperors had
confirmed cruelty as a ground for divorce, saying
that beating was " unfit for free women."
Justinian and his clerical advisers, however,
thought otherwise, and he specifically abolished
the right of the wife to a divorce on that ground.
Earlier Emperors had also laid down, in conformity with the old law, that where the husband
was banished, the marriage was not thereby
dissolved " if the calamity which had befallen
the husband had not changed the affection of
the wife." Justinian abolished this also, and
compelled the wife to remain married in name.
If the husband was absent for a long time without news being heard of him, the period of

waiting which the wife was compelled to undergo was extended to ten years.

The grounds upon which a husband might divorce his wife were abortion, adultery or suspicion of adultery. Adultery was presumed in the case of the wife whenever she, without her husband's permission, went to the theatre or circus, dined out with another man, spent a night away from home, or indulged in mixed bathing. Grounds common to both were impotence, which appears to have been introduced for the first time as a ground for divorce by Justinian, an attempt upon the life of either of the spouses by the other, the taking of vows of chastity by entering a monastery, which, being "the better life," was regarded as " civil death," and captivity or absence for ten years without being heard of. Where a mistake was made in some essential particular, *e.g.*, if the wife who had been thought to be free turned out to be a slave, the marriage was regarded as never having taken place at all. The innocent party to a divorce was entitled to the custody of the children, whom both were bound to maintain according to their means, but if the wife married again, the husband, though he might be the guilty party, was allowed the custody of the children. Inter-

34

marriage between adulterers was forbidden, and if the wife committed adultery she was condemned to celibacy for five years, as she had "shown herself unworthy of marriage," and if she did marry during that period she was declared to be infamous. If the wife divorced her husband without a reasonable cause as defined by the law, she had to go to a monastery for life, and her goods went partly to the bishop and partly to the children. No condemnation to chastity was, however, laid down for the husband in the like cases. A promise by a married woman to marry another man during the lifetime of her husband had been allowed to be a ground for divorce by previous Imperial legislation, but Justinian, while punishing the wife in such cases, ordered that the marriage tie must remain in force.*

The "pious austerity" of Justinian, however, was not satisfied with emphasising the carnal element of marriage and the subjection of married women to their husbands. He indicated the tendency of all this legislation by inventing the enforcement of chastity not only in the case of married women who were recalcitrant, but in the case of all who divorced one another by

* Cod. 5, 17 ; Novels 22 and 117 ; Brouwer, ch. 31 ; Pothier Pandectae, 22 and 24, 2 ; Leo, Novel 30.

mutual consent. Divorce by mutual consent had never been disturbed by any previous Emperor, and had been re-affirmed by Anastasius a few years before. Justinian enacted that where divorce took place by mutual consent, the parties, unless they did so for the sake of chastity by voluntarily retiring to monasteries, were to be thrust into monasteries for the rest of their days, and must forfeit their property in favour of the monasteries and of their children. If either or both made the taking of religious vows a pretext for divorce, and afterwards returned to the world and married again or " lived luxuriously," they had to forfeit whatever property remained in their possession to the children, or, if there were no children, to the State. In all these cases, however, the divorce was not declared illegal, for it was divorce, " though they die in prison." This interference with the remnants of Roman liberty by the peopling of monasteries and the enrichment of the Church by the unhappiness of married people did not remain in force long. Not only did this law create great popular discontent, but it was found that all this enforced celibacy did not improve either morality or peace within or without the convent walls, and it was accordingly repealed by Justin, the nephew and successor of Justinian, who also restored a large measure of religious toleration, in the first year of his reign (565 A.D.).*

Justin, in restoring divorce by mutual consent, said that this law of his " pious father," and the penalties which it entailed, were " not applicable to our time," and he had therefore re-enacted " the present sacred law by which we lay down that, as formerly, marriage can be dissolved by mutual consent. . . . For if mutual affection is the basis of marriage, it is right that when the parties have changed their minds, they should be allowed to dissolve it by mutual consent." In the preamble to this novel the Emperor said that many married persons had come to him who said that they hated one another and could not live together. Their married life consisted of a constant and regular warfare of words and blows, and, although they could not set up any of the recognised grounds for divorce which had been defined by previous Emperors, they wished to be divorced. He had advised them to become reconciled, and had even used threats and postponed divorce for a time so that they might have an opportunity of doing so ; but in vain ; for it had been found to be extremely difficult to reconcile those who hated one another, and even the fact of their

* Novels 134 & 140 ; Bryce, *Studies in History and Jurisprudence*, II, xvi.

having children was not sufficient to induce them to live in harmony together. In some cases they had even gone as far as to make attempts upon each other's lives.*

So the law remained, and other grounds for divorce were added by succeeding Emperors, until the end of the Empire. The Emperor Leo, at the beginning of the tenth century, who, like his predecessors, considered that in all his legislation he was "following the Holy Spirit," in many of his novels quoted the first chapter of Genesis, the well-known text of Paul, and other Scriptural texts as to the origin and object of marriage. Following the prevailing interpretations of these passages by the ecclesiastics of this time, he forbade the marriage of eunuchs and the contracting of third, as another Emperor (Zeno) forbade the contracting of fourth marriages. The value of women in the matrimonial market and their rights when married had by this time reached a very low ebb. Leo considered that it was " not difficult to find a partner for life," but it undoubtedly was extremely difficult for a woman to escape from a hateful or intolerable union. Leo, however, made the lot of woman somewhat easier by

---

* Novel 140, "Si namque mutua affectio matrimonia conficit, merito diversa voluntas eadem per consensum dirimit."

enacting that where a married woman during her marriage promised to marry another man the husband was allowed to divorce her. The Emperor points out how Justinian contradicted himself by not allowing divorce in such a case, while condemning the woman to undergo certain penalties. Leo, however, while inflicting upon the wife certain pecuniary penalties, allowed her her freedom from an intolerable bond, for to allow a wife to talk treason with another man was as intolerable as the recitation of a treasonable ode in a theatre. As God had joined them together in "one flesh," the wife who "tore herself from the limb to which she was joined," and turned her eyes towards another man with wanton intention, was guilty of contempt for the Creator, who had joined them, while there could be no better evidence than this of hostility towards her husband.*

The same Emperor, however, in his two latest laws, made some instructive observations upon the Scriptural texts, showing that even the most dogmatic of the Emperors considered that those texts were capable of a more liberal interpretation than that which had been put upon them by ecclesiastics. Two cases had arisen, in one of which a husband, and in the other a

* Leo, Novels 30, 31, 33, 90, 91, 98 ; Zeno, *Constitutiones*, 2.

wife, applied to the Emperor for leave to dissolve their respective marriages on the ground of the insanity of their spouses, and to marry again without incurring the penalties which had been laid down by Church and State. The Emperor granted the applications, and, in laying down insanity as a valid ground for divorce in the future, he began by quoting the first chapter of Genesis and saying that marriage was intended for the preservation of the human race and for the mutual aid and happiness of the spouses, and not for their mutual affliction and misery. The condemnation of the one to remain married to the other in spite of that other's insanity could not therefore reasonably be expected, for no one could be so harsh as to shut up anyone with a wild beast or one who had lost his reason. But it had been said that by marriage the two became " one flesh," and that each member ought to endure all the diseases of the other, and the Divine precept was that those whom God had joined should not be separated. Those were excellent and indeed Divine words, seeing that they were pronounced by God Himself. But they were not in point in that case, nor were they cited in accordance with the intention of their Divine author. For if marriage always remained in the same condition as it was when it began, whoever separated himself from it would indeed be wicked, and would not escape censure. But here the husband could not even hear the human voice of his wife, or receive from her any of those blessings which she had showered upon him during the days of their happiness. If the insanity had arisen before marriage, it would have rendered the marriage null and void, but as the same calamity had arisen after marriage it rendered the marriage equally useless in effect. Although, therefore, insanity had not been laid down by previous Emperors as a ground for divorce, the grounds which they had laid down, such as impotence, religious differences, and prodigality on the part of the husband, were not to be compared with insanity. Where the husband or wife was hopelessly insane, the divorce injured no one. By granting a divorce on that ground he was not abrogating the laws, but merely extending them by interpretation to meet cases of that kind. As to the argument that the two were " one flesh " because of the religious ceremony, and therefore ought not to be separated, and that one member of the same body, especially when that member was the husband who was said to be the head, could not be amputated even though attacked

41

by disease, this appeared to him to miss the whole purpose of the benediction of the marriage ceremony. The object of that benediction was to bestow the greatest blessings upon the married pair, to consecrate their chastity and their future progeny by joining them in indissoluble bonds of love. But how could insanity be made to fit in with this integrity of chastity when the husband could not even recognise his unfortunate wife ? How could children be hoped for when insanity exhibited to the wretched wife the horrible spectacle of a more wretched husband, with whom she could not live ? By what bond of love were they joined when disease brutalised the whole man into something which was not human ? Not only was there a grave danger of the transmission of insanity to the children, but the sane spouse, who desired to marry again, should not be prevented from doing so by an intolerable calamity which arose through no fault of his own. Divorce in such a case was neither inconsistent with the marriage ceremony nor in any respect criminal.*

These novels, which are the last words uttered by any Roman Emperor on the subject of divorce, show that in spite of the influence which the Church had had upon the law of divorce, and

* Leo, Novels 111-112.

in spite of the fact that a celibate clergy, whose temporal power became stronger as the Empire declined, interfered on every possible occasion to enforce the retention of the outward form of marriage, regardless of the wishes, welfare or affections of those who were married, the Emperors repudiated the sacramental conception of marriage as a legal dogma, and held that the Scriptures were not inconsistent with the Roman idea of marriage, and above all with divorce by mutual consent, or where all affection between the parties had ceased. The desire to regard the wishes and welfare of the parties as the test of divorce is carefully expressed by the Emperors throughout the whole of their legislation, though in some cases it became a mere formula and a pretext for restricting the rights of the parties. Theodosius and Valentinian, who codified the grounds for divorce (which had been laid down by previous Emperors beginning with Constantine), apologised for the restriction of the right of divorce on the pretext that the interests of the children should be protected. They expressed their desire, however, " to set free by the necessary assistance of the law, however unfortunate the occasion might be, those who were oppressed by necessity." Even Justinian, the greatest dogmatist of them all, said that the grounds for divorce which he defined were "reasonable grounds," although it is clear that the supposed pretext of protecting the children had disappeared when he condemned the parties to remain for life imprisoned in monasteries.*

In the long struggle between liberty and dogma—the people having no voice in the determination of either—dogma had left almost indelible traces upon the law of divorce. The arbitrary differentiation between the rights of husband and wife, the subjection of married women, the abolition of a married woman's protection by the right of divorce from the brutality or misconduct of her husband, the beginning of what afterwards became judicial separation by the enforced chastity of one or both of the spouses, and above all the association of divorce with crime ; these, which in the Roman law merely accompanied the undoubted right of divorce by the parties without the necessity of any inquiry into the causes of divorce, were the germs which were soon to grow into a law which declared marriage to be indissoluble. "The doctrine of indissolubility," as a learned authority says, "was ingrafted on the law, not by the wise men who at any time swayed the civil

* Cod. 5, 17, 8 ; Novels 22, 4 and 117, 9.

affairs of Rome, but by the Roman Church as a religious tenet." We now pass into the period known as the Dark Ages, in which this tenet was to become the dominating rule of law for one half of Europe, while in the other half divorce was associated only with crimes which were generally those which the Emperors had defined; in which the affections, wishes and welfare of mankind were crushed in a terrible machine of spiritual and temporal power. "To pass from the civil law of Rome to the ecclesiastical law of the Dark and Middle Ages," says Mr. Bryce, "is like quitting an open country, intersected by good roads, for a tract of mountain and forest where rough and tortuous paths furnish the only means of transit." *

* Bishop, § 24 ; Bryce, p. 416 and foll.

THE EASTERN CHURCH AND
EASTERN EUROPE

IV

THE EASTERN CHURCH AND EASTERN EUROPE

"The restoration of the Western Empire by Charlemagne was speedily followed by the separation of the Greek and Latin Churches. A religious and national animosity still pervades the two largest communions of the Christian world."—GIBBON.

THE final rupture between the Churches of the East and West took place in the middle of the eleventh century, when Pope Gregory VII, the same who interdicted the marriage of the clergy, excommunicated the Eastern Church. Since that time two diametrically opposite systems of divorce have been put into practice in the two halves of Europe by the two Churches. The Eastern Church, which still calls itself the Orthodox Church, contains the oldest communion of the Christian Church, and operates over those regions which were the scenes of the early apostolic missions, never adopted, as an essential part of its dogma, the celibate view of life to the extent which that view was adopted and enforced by the Western

Church. From the time of the Council of Nicæa, over which Constantine presided, priests have been allowed to marry. Nor did the Eastern Church regard the sacraments as indelible, for priests have always been allowed to resign their priesthood and become laymen, while the sacrament of marriage has always been regarded as dissoluble. A married clergy in the East has always been more tolerant towards those whose married lives were unhappy or intolerable, than a celibate clergy which laid down laws for others to observe. It does not appear that the view of the Eastern Church on the subject of divorce was one of the causes of the schism between the two Churches. On the contrary, the Catholic Church has always tolerated the heresy of the Eastern Church, and has never regarded its own views upon divorce as essential to salvation. Even by the Council of Trent, in 1563, the Catholic Church arrived at a verbal compromise with a view to conciliating the Eastern Church, on the Venetian ambassador representing to it that divorce was allowed by those who followed the Greek Church. The Council contented itself with saying, not that marriage was indissoluble, but that " if any one said that the Church erred " in maintaining that the sacrament of marriage was indissoluble, he should be condemned to everlasting punishment (*anathema sit.*).*

By the Eastern Church " divorce was regarded as compatible with the Scriptural command that 'man shall not put asunder those whom God has joined together,' because the decree of divorce was regarded merely as a legal recognition that marriage no longer subsisted between the spouses." This view of the Scriptures was not in conflict with the Roman law, and that law as it had been modified by Justinian was accordingly adopted by the Eastern Church. The omission of the novel of Justin restoring divorce by mutual consent, by Leo in the tenth century, when he ordered the whole of the Roman law to be translated into Greek, appears to be mainly responsible for the fact that divorce by mutual consent was not adopted by the episcopal courts of the Eastern Church. Whether that novel was omitted by the authority of the Emperor or was due to the ecclesiastics who translated it, after the decline of the Empire when the bishops obtained exclusive jurisdiction over divorce, in the East, as in the West, divorce by mutual consent was not allowed. The necessity of a judicial trial of all divorce cases which the

* Gibbon, ch. ix; Stanley, *Lectures on the Eastern Church esp.* Lectures I-IV ; Lea, *History of the Inquisition*, III, ch. ix ; Burge (1910), iii, p. 810 ; Pothier, *Mariage*, § 497.

Church gradually laid down, and the power which the Church thereby obtained over the intimate affairs of the family, would clearly have been nullified if the Church had allowed the parties themselves to have the deciding voice in divorce. Marriage being called a sacrament or spiritual matter for the purposes of this exclusive jurisdiction, the weakness of the temporal authorities and the absence of the voice of the people in legislation perpetuated this episcopal jurisdiction over divorce, which remains to this day in Russia and Servia, while in other Eastern countries, although the secular courts have obtained jurisdiction in more recent times, it is still necessary for the courts to have a report upon the case by the ecclesiastical authorities to the effect that they have been unable to effect a reconciliation between the parties.*

The episcopal courts, obtaining exclusive jurisdiction over divorce, took as the basis of their law the grounds for divorce which had been defined by Justinian in his novels, which, as we have seen, included impotence, an attempt upon the life of one by the other, long absence, abortion, the taking of monastic vows, treason and other crimes, and adultery, with

* Brouwer, 31, 12; Burge (1910), iii, 811-2 and 840-4; Reports on the Laws of Marriage and Divorce in Foreign Countries (1894), Part II, pp. 75, 129, 135.

all the inequalities of those laws between husband and wife especially as regards adultery and the penalties which the wife had to undergo, and the restrictions against remarriage in certain cases. These laws remain in force in Servia and Greece. Thus in Greece " attending theatres, races, or shooting expeditions against the will or without the knowledge of the husband," and various other acts of independence on the part of the wife from which adultery is presumed, afford a good ground for divorce to the husband. In the same country it is still necessary, where adultery is the ground of the action, for the wife to prove that the adultery of the husband took place with a married woman and under certain aggravating circumstances. The Eastern Church, however, gradually, by interpretation, added other grounds for divorce, such as religious differences between the parties, e.g., where one of them became a heretic or an infidel. Spiritual relationship created by baptism was regarded as an impediment to marriage and a ground for divorce, while if the husband became a bishop his wife was entitled to sue for a divorce on that ground. These grounds are still in force in Servia.*

Secular legislation and interpretation have

* *Ibid.* pp. 75, 135.

considerably modified the Canon laws of the
Eastern Church and in some respects tempered
their harshness.   Thus in Greece it has been held
that the wife no longer forfeits her dowry and a
great part of her property to her husband in
the event of her adultery.   This forfeiture had
been devised by Justinian mainly to prevent
women from obtaining divorces, and had been
confirmed by Leo,* as a consolation for the
husband in such a case, while the wife had been
condemned either to perpetual exile or imprisonment in a monastery.   In Russia and Roumania
husband and wife have been placed on the
same footing as regards all the grounds for
divorce.   The grounds for divorce which have
been introduced by secular legislation in all
these States, some of which, but not all, are
recognised by the Church, are desertion or
refusal to perform marital duties, the commission of certain crimes, leprosy, insanity and
invincible repugnance or incompatibility of
temper.   In Russia where one of the parties
has been condemned to banishment the other
is not bound to follow if he or she does not
choose to do so, but may sue for a divorce;
thus in this respect the important principle of
the Roman law has been retained.†

* Leo, Novel 32.   † Reports on the Laws of Marriage and
Divorce in Foreign Countries (1894), Part II, pp. 75, 126, 129.

Although, therefore, mutual consent is not recognised as a ground for divorce except in Roumania, where its introduction as well as divorce on the ground of cruelty has been due to the influence of the Code Napoléon, the wishes and welfare of the parties are to a great extent considered, and the reason why divorce by mutual consent was not retained was, as we have seen, due solely to an historical accident. " In the absence of any check upon collusion, undefended actions for divorce often amount to the same thing," says Burge, referring to Greece. In Russia members of other Churches than the Orthodox are allowed to divorce each other in their own ecclesiastical courts on whatever grounds those Churches allow. Thus Jews in Russia are allowed divorce by mutual consent with the permission of the Rabbi, according to the Jewish law.*

As divorce has always been recognised by the Eastern Church, judicial separation has never been adopted except in some cases as a preliminary to divorce. Divorce, however, is refused where both parties are equally guilty, a doctrine which was never recognised by the Roman law, by which, as we have seen, divorce was not an action at law but a private matter.

* *Ibid.* pp. 126, 129.

The restrictions against the remarriage of one of the parties either for a time or for ever, and the forbidding of inter-marriage between adulterers, has been retained in nearly all the laws of Eastern Europe owing to the influence of the Church, though the provision of other grounds for divorce besides adultery has rendered these restrictions for the most part obsolete. Marriage by the laws of all these States is now defined as a civil contract, with the exception of Russia, where it is still styled a sacrament, and the laws of divorce in all these countries are all regulated by secular legislation. Thus in the East of Europe the Imperial Roman law has always remained in force, and, although it was for a long time administered by a Church which has always allowed divorce according to its rules, provided the parties first obtained the sanction of the Church, the tendency has been, as popular liberty has increased, to return to the principles of the original Roman law.

V

THE CANON LAW AND WESTERN EUROPE IN THE MIDDLE AGES

Per questo l'Evangelio e i dottor magni
Son derelitto, e solo ai Decretali
Si studia sì che pare ai lor vivagni
A questo intende il papa e i cardinali :
Non vanno i lor pensieri a Nazzarette.

DANTE, " Paradiso," xix, 133.

Therefore it is the Gospel and great Doctors are deserted, and only the Decretals are studied, as may be seen upon their margins. Thereon the Popes and Cardinals are intent ; ne'er wend their thoughts to Nazareth.

Rev. P. H. WICKSTEED's translation.

IN Western Europe the Catholic Church had an earlier and an even more comprehensive grasp over marriage and divorce than the Eastern Church. As the authority of the Emperors declined in Italy, a succession of strong Popes, who were monks and lawyers, made effective use of the prevailing anarchy by consolidating their power. They issued Decretals, in which they gave their decisions upon all kinds of spiritual and temporal matters which had been referred to them by the faithful for their spiritual advice, and these Decretals soon came to take the place of Imperial laws and to be observed as binding upon all Christians, being considered by the subordinate ecclesiastics as " of greater weight than Scripture." In the twelfth century, Gratian, a monk and lawyer of the great law school at Bologna, published an authoritative collection of these " Decretals," some of which were spurious, but all extolling the supremacy of the Church in all matters, together with commentaries in the form of canons of the Church councils, passages from the Bible, the Fathers and the Roman law. Cujas, one of the greatest commentators upon the Roman law, says that " the papal lawyers used the Roman law to adorn their Decretals, and all that is of excellence in the Canon law is borrowed from it." Later collections of Decretals were made by the authority of various Popes, such as Innocent III, Gregory IX, Boniface VIII, and Clement V, and this body of law became known as the Canon law. As Christianity spread over Western Europe the bishops, to whom, like the Popes, large tracts of land were granted, over which they exercised both feudal and spiritual jurisdiction, administered this law in their local courts, and were thus enabled to mould an ignorant and superstitious people to the supreme will of the Church. Strong and weak kings alike, such as Charlemagne and William the Conqueror and their weak successors, handed over to the exclusive jurisdiction of the Church, in exchange for its blessing, all the rights and liberties of their subjects in the most intimate concerns of their daily life, not only in marriage and divorce, but in a great number of other subjects, such as wills, which were all treated by the Church as spiritual matters. Besides the bishops who exercised this wide and ever-increasing jurisdiction in their local courts, legates and other agents of the Popes obtained, often by purchase, the right of deciding certain cases, coupled with the power of excommunication and other penances, which were the ordinary means of enforcing the decrees of the ecclesiastical courts. The royal courts, whose officials were either ecclesiastics or the servants of despotic monarchs, enforced the ecclesiastical sentences by the severest temporal penalties. Pope Gregory IX, the founder of the Inquisition, was one of the principal founders of the Canon law. The Inquisition, indeed, which had a strong influence upon all civil and criminal procedure, and in a great measure was responsible for the grip which the Canon law obtained, was put into force in the holy Roman Empire early in the thirteenth century by Frederick II, who was an agnostic and the "arch-enemy of the Church," although he desired to obtain its favour, and the same Emperor about the same time declared the Canon law to be binding over the whole of the Empire. Thus marriage and divorce were placed in *mortmain* for many centuries, and monks and priests, whose lives were devoted to an enforced celibacy which was not always accompanied by the "gift of chastity," found a constant and profitable employment in deciding sexual problems in public tribunals, which were a combination of the confessional and the Inquisition, and to which all unhappy spouses who wished to be freed from each other's society were compelled to have recourse.*

By the Canon law marriage was declared to be indissoluble. Charlemagne, the first Emperor of the holy Roman Empire, who was

---

* H. C. Lea, *Hist. of the Inquisition*, I, ch. i, and pp. 320-1 ; Pollock and Maitland, *Hist. of English Law*, I, iv ; Rittershusius, *Differentiarum Juris*, pr. ; Arntzenius, *Inst. Jur. Belg.*, pr., I, §§ 3-11 ; Burn, *Eccles. Law* (1824), *s.v.* "Courts" & "Excommunication" ; Blok, *Hist. of the Netherlands* (Putnam), vol. I ; Jacob Voorda, *Interpretationes* (1735) ; Harnack, *Hist. of Dogma*, pp. 382-414 ; Lea, *Studies in Church History*, pp. 159 and foll., where that learned author says that the divorce of the Empress Teutberga may be taken as "the foundation of that papal omnipotence which was to overshadow Christendom." See also Gratian, 27.2.26 ; 32.2.24.

crowned by the Pope in the year 800, was the
first of many a temporal ruler who, as Mr. Lecky
says, "declared marriage to be indissoluble,
and pronounced divorce to be criminal, but he
did not venture to make it penal, and he practised it himself." This also represents the
practice of the Church, for no sooner was
marriage made indissoluble by the Canon law
than the Popes began to devise ingenious ex-
pedients for dissolving it, and for separating
those "whom God had joined." Marriage was
declared to be a sacrament, although it was
formed by consent alone, no "vows" or
religious ceremony being requisite or customary
for its celebration during the whole of the
Middle Ages. Marriage is defined by Gratian
as the spiritual union, constituted by the will of
the parties, which the physical consummation
confirms and perfects. The grounds for calling
marriage a sacrament need not be closely inquired
into, because it is clear, as Pothier, himself a
Catholic, says, that the papal lawyers insisted
upon this in order that the Pope might obtain
exclusive temporal jurisdiction over it. The
material of the sacrament, he says, is the
contract or consent of the parties, and when this
contract has been dissolved by the secular
power the sacrament ceases to exist. The usual

explanation given by the Canon lawyers for
calling marriage a sacrament is that it is said
to represent the indissoluble union between
Christ and the Church, according to the analogy
given by St. Paul. Of this the celebrated
Cardinal Cajetan said that marriage according
to St. Paul was not a sacrament but a mystery,
and the mystery of these words was great.
Brouwer asks how marriage can be a sacrament
when its most essential element consists in a
work of the flesh. The attempt to translate
the parables and analogies of the Bible into
positive laws is characteristic of the whole of
the Canon law, for the jurisdiction of the Pope
in these matters rested upon well-known passages in the Gospels, such as the words of Peter,
" Behold here are two swords," the swords
being said to be respectively the spiritual and
temporal power, while the words, " Know ye
not that we shall judge angels ? " were considered
to be applicable with greater force to the
jurisdiction of the Church over merely secular
matters. The greater the mystery in the
Biblical words, the greater were the pretensions
of the papal lawyers to exercise jurisdiction over
such matters. The text in St. Matthew saying
that adultery could be committed by the mind
alone was applied by them to a case in which a

wife or husband, while performing their marital duties, were occupied with the thought of another man or woman, and it was decided that this was adultery.*

Following the Scriptural texts, especially those of St. Matthew, divorce was allowed by the Canon law on the ground of "fornication"; the parties were not allowed to marry again, but must live in celibacy or be reconciled because they are "one flesh," and because the sacrament is indelible even though both parties have been excommunicated, "for God never dies." If either party after divorce married again, it was adultery. The only divorce allowable according to this theory was separation from bed and board or judicial separation. But it is clear that this rigid doctrine was never strictly maintained. In a great number of cases the separation operated as a dissolution of the marriage, for the hope of reconciliation was in most cases a fiction, while the Church often pronounced a permanent separation between the parties and did not greatly concern itself with what happened to them afterwards. If either of them married again or lived in

* Lecky, *Hist. of European Morals*, II, 352 ; Pothier, *Mariage*, I, 3 ; Grat. Decret. 27, 1 & 27, 2, 26 ; Harnack, *Hist. of Dogma*, pp. 468-9 and 487 ; Rittershusius, *pr.* ; Grat. Decret. 4, 17, 13 ; Brouwer I, 9 & II, 18.

adultery, their crime was only a minor one which was subject to light penances. The discretion of the bishops and the dispensing power of the Popes was practically unlimited, and by the omission by the bishop, on pronouncing the divorce, of the injunction that the parties were not to marry again, the Church frequently connived at re-marriage, especially where the parties were wealthy or powerful.*

But it was soon found that the interpretation of "fornication" to mean adultery was not sufficient for the growing practice of the papal courts. This flexible and doubtful term was therefore interpreted to mean heresy and infidelity, which were said to be equivalent to idolatry, which again was spiritual adultery, and even worse than physical adultery. Religious differences of this nature therefore between the parties became valid grounds for divorce. This interpretation was strengthened by the application of the well-known text of St. Paul, which said that if the unbelieving spouse departed he should be allowed to depart, for the faithful spouse was not bound in such a case, for we were called to peace—a text which afterwards served the Reformers in the like case

---

* Grat. Decret. 27, 2, 1 & 29 ; 32, 7, 1-2 & *ibid. causs.* 27-33 *passim* ; Greg. Decret. 4, 11 & 15 ; 4, 17, 13.

to establish their doctrine of malicious desertion. St. Augustine was relied upon as having said that the limb which scandalised the husband or wife should be amputated—a striking illustration of the idea of divorce being a surgical operation which lay at the root of the Canon law of divorce. For a long time, therefore, religious differences between the parties, *e.g.*, where one was a pagan, a heretic, or a Jew, were treated as dissolving marriage. Pope Innocent III later substituted permanent separation for divorce in such cases, because it was alleged that many spouses simulated heresy in order to obtain divorce. When the Inquisition came into constant operation a false accusation would often serve as a divorce, as heresy was punished by death, and a charge of heresy rarely ended in the discharge of the accused person. A case is given by Mr. Lea in which a husband was accused of heresy before the Inquisition, the principal informant being his wife, who was proved to have been living with another man, and to have " wished her husband dead that she might marry a certain Pug Oler," and to have declared " that she would willingly become a leper if that would bring it about." In spite of this, the husband did not escape. Mr. Lecky says of another of the spheres of activity of the Inquisi-

67

tion in bringing about divorces: " Sometimes a husband attempted in the witch courts to cut the tie which the Church had pronounced indissoluble, and numbers of wives have in consequence perished at the stake." The taking of monastic vows frequently operated as a cause of divorce, although later a distinction was drawn between a marriage which had been consummated and one which had not. If the marriage had not been consummated, divorce in such a case was allowed, because the two had not become " one flesh," even though the sacrament had been celebrated in church. If, however, the marriage had been consummated, divorce was not allowed even where one of the parties retired to a monastery, for the two had become " one flesh " and how, it was asked, could one part of the same body go to a monastery while the other remained in the world ? The parties could, however, by mutual consent retire to separate monasteries and thereby dissolve the marriage, for in such a case it was God who separated them. The taking of formal vows of chastity by one or both parties soon became a recognised and convenient manner of obtaining a divorce.*

* Grat. Decret. 28 ; Greg. Decret. 4, 19, 6 ; Lea, *Hist. of the Inquisition*, I, p. 448; Lecky, *Hist. of Rationalism*, I, p. 23 ; Grat. Decret. 11, 3, 3 ; 27, 2, 24-26 ; 33, 2, 4 ; Pothier, *Mariage*, §§ 468-470 ; Froude, *Life and Letters of Erasmus*, p. 376 (1906 ed.),

THE WESTERN CHURCH

Once the Church had established its claim to exclusive jurisdiction over divorce, it began to divorce persons upon grounds which did not even purport to be based upon the Scriptures, but upon purely human grounds. An attempt upon the life of one of the parties by the other was recognised as a good ground for the dissolution of marriage by a council of the Church in the year 870, and the innocent party was allowed to marry again. It was, however, laid down some centuries later by one of the Popes that where the wife attempted to take the life of her husband, only a separation could be granted; the husband was not allowed to marry again until after the death of the wife, while the wife was forbidden the right of re-marriage for life. The long absence of either spouse was sometimes held to be a good ground for divorce in the episcopal courts; this practice receiving papal sanction. Excessive cruelty was a good ground for separation, but no remedy was granted where one of the spouses became insane or suffered from some intolerable or contagious disease, such as leprosy. Pope Alexander III wrote to a King of Aragon: "Since husband and wife are one flesh, we command that wives must follow their husbands who are lepers, and husbands their wives." Where a husband was suffering from a loathsome disease the French judges, following the Canon law, held that this was not cruelty to the wife even where the disease had been communicated to her by her husband, and gave her no remedy. She was ordered to leave a convent to which she had retired to escape his loathsome embraces, and return to him.*

Marriage, though called a sacrament, was in practice treated by the Canon lawyers as a contract based upon the consent or will of the parties, followed by consummation. Where, therefore, consummation was impossible for physical reasons, or there was some mistake or defect in the consent or will of the parties, the marriage was dissolved and both parties were allowed to marry again. The remedy for this, which came to be known as a declaration of nullity of marriage, on the fiction that the marriage had never taken place even though it had been celebrated in church and the parties had lived together and borne children for years, was specifically known as divorce in the Canon law. The parties were restored to their original condition by *restitutio in integrum* so far as the Church could physically do so,

* Grat. Decret. 6, 31, 1 ; Greg. Decret. 4, 19, 1 ; Leyser, § 315 ; Pothier, *Mariage*, § 514, and Maître Paillet's note ; Rittershusius II.

while the children became illegitimate. Thus impotence was a good ground for the dissolution of the sacrament—" an egregious ground," as Bynkershoek says, " worthy in dignity to a sacrament." Sometimes this impotence was considered by the Church to be caused by sorcery, and when " exorcisms and prayers and almsgiving and other ecclesiastical remedies proved powerless for three years to overcome the power of Satan," the Church dissolved the indissoluble sacrament. " Such a cause was alleged," Mr. Lea tells us, " when Philip Augustus abandoned his bride, Ingeburga of Denmark . . . and Bishop Durand in his Speculum Juris tells us that these cases were of daily occurrence." The parties in such cases had to endure the indignity of a physical examination, the wife being examined by a jury of matrons. Cases of divorce on the ground of impotence are reported in the " Decretals," in one of which a woman after divorce on the ground of her alleged impotence married again, and it was discovered " by some miracle " that she was not impotent as far as her second husband was concerned. She was accordingly ordered to return to her first husband, though the Pope raised a doubt as to whether the vows which she had taken on her second marriage did not stand

71

in the way of this. In a similar case in England in Elizabeth's reign it was held that the divorce was valid and that the second marriage was only voidable on the ground of fraud. To such shifts were unhappy spouses obliged to resort in order to obtain release from a hateful marriage.*

As mistake or fraud vitiated consent, these became recognised as grounds for dissolving the sacrament. The mistake might be made by one of the parties or by the priest who celebrated the marriage turning out to be a layman. The discovery of a husband after the marriage that his wife had been unchaste before marriage was held to be a sufficient ground for divorce. The fraud which Laban had practised upon Jacob and the mistake which the latter had made were not considered as being in point in the more perfect world in which the monks who decided these cases moved. Similarly, the rule made by one of the Popes that no one should be allowed to marry one whom he had " polluted by adultery " was not considered to conflict with the case of David and Bathsheba, from whose union Solomon was born.†

But the most usual ground for divorce by the

* Grat. Decret. 27, 2, 150, and Greg. Decret. IV, 15 ; Burn, *Eccles. Law* (1824), vol. II, pp. 500-502.

† Decret. Grat. 29, 1, and 31, 1-10.

Canon law was where some forbidden degree of relationship existed between the parties. Marriages had been forbidden by the Church between blood relations so far back as memory could go. This was afterwards interpreted to mean relationship within the seventh and at a much later date within the fourth degree, the canonical degrees being much wider than those of the civil law.* The same rule was applied to relationship by marriage, or affinity, where there was no real relationship at all, for as by marriage the parties became " one flesh," all their relatives by blood and affinity became equally related to one another. To this wide scheme of relationship was added a new kind of relationship called spiritual, for by such sacraments as baptism and confirmation, the recipient of the sacrament was said to be " born again " and therefore became related to his sponsors, the officiating priest, and all their relatives. Where such a wide list of impediments to marriage existed — to which were added many other impediments which were all committed to memory, together with the principal rules of the Canon law, by the monks by means

* The computation of collateral degrees in the Civil law was made by reckoning back to the common ancestor and then down again, while in the Canon law it was only back to the common ancestor. Thus in the Civil law second cousins were related in the sixth degree, while in the Canon law they were related in the third degree.

73

of sonorous doggerel verses—it is obvious that many who found themselves so related would wish to intermarry, especially as no real relationship in most cases existed between them. Hence arose the necessity of purchasing dispensations, and it is the common observation of historians and lawyers that all these impediments were " providentially discovered " by the Popes for the entrapping of humanity, and especially for the purpose of obtaining revenue when they could not do so by direct taxation. " Even more demoralising," says Mr. Lea in the *Cambridge Modern History*, " were the revenues derived from the sale of countless dispensations for marriage within the prohibited degrees . . . so that its prescriptions might almost seem to have been framed for the purpose of enabling the Holy See to profit by their violation." The same writer quotes a mediæval authority as saying that " the most holy sacrament of marriage, owing to the remote consanguinity coming within the prohibited degrees, was made a subject of derision to the laity by the venality with which marriages were made and unmade to fill the pouches of the episcopal officials." Cardinal Borgia, who was Vice-Chancellor of Pope Innocent III, when reproved for the open sale of pardons replied that " God desired not the death of sinners, but that they should pay and live." Dispensations even where they had been obtained were often a frequent source of litigation and considerable profit to the papal lawyers whenever either of the parties wished for a divorce and accordingly began to doubt the validity of their dispensation. Where no dispensation had been obtained, the parties, when they found their married life unhappy or intolerable, began to investigate their pedigrees, and were unlucky if they could discover no impediment sufficient to establish the right of divorce.*

A typical case of divorce on this ground is that of the Earl of Bothwell, who, wishing to divorce his wife in order that he might marry Mary, Queen of Scots, obtained a divorce under the Canon law on the ground that one of his ancestors had married into his wife's family nearly a century before. In that case a dispensation had actually been obtained, but this fact was conveniently ignored by both parties and by the court at the trial. Another famous case is that of the Countess Jacqueline of Holland in the fifteenth century. Wishing to marry

* Lea, *Hist. of the Inquisition*, I, p. 21, and III, pp. 643-4. and in *Camb. Mod. Hist.*, ch. xix; Jacob Voorda, in an inaugural address at Utrecht (1735); Rittershusius I, ix; Pollock & Maitland II; Bryce, *Studies in Hist. & Jurisprudence*, II, p. 421.

her cousin, John of Brabant, she requested a dispensation from the Pope, which was promised, and even sent, but recalled on the eve of the marriage. As the marriage turned out unfortunate for her, she afterwards wished to obtain a divorce on the ground of relationship, but as her husband by the divorce would have lost the rich province of Holland, the latter brought considerable influence to bear upon the Pope, who, notwithstanding the fact that he had previously refused a dispensation, declared the marriage to be valid and indissoluble. Jacqueline was married again to the Duke Humphrey of Gloucester, who also deserted her. In spite of all this, however, her first marriage was declared valid. The case of Henry VIII and his divorce from Catherine of Aragon is well known, while Napoleon, who divorced Josephine because of some flaw in the dispensation and because he had never given his inward consent to the marriage, pleaded the example of no less than thirteen French kings who had divorced their queens on similar pretexts.*

Matrimony was said by Pope Gregory IX, the founder of the Inquisition and one of the principal authors of the Canon law, to be so

---

* H. Graham, *A Group of Scottish Women*, p. 41 & foll. ; Blok, *Hist. of the Netherlands*, I.

called because the mother's part in it was
" onerous, dolorous and laborious." The position of married women under the Canon law was
entirely in accordance with this sonorous sentence, her position being one of subjection
from which, when it turned out to be unhappy,
there was no escape. The husband was regarded
as her " head," to whom she owed unquestioning
obedience, in return for a protection and love
which were not always forthcoming. By virtue
of his divine right and superiority the husband
had the right of chastising and imprisoning her.
As his evidence was generally preferred to hers,
even in the rare cases where she was in a position
to obtain evidence of his misconduct or independent evidence of his ill-treatment, she
was practically without a remedy, for she was
compelled first of all to restore to the husband
possession of herself and to return to his
authority if she had left him on account of his
conduct. The Popes themselves recognised
that for a wife to obtain evidence of her husband's
misconduct was practically impossible, while
in her own case she was subject to the closest
supervision. The superior courts of all countries refused to grant a wife even a separation
on the ground of her husband's adultery alone,
for the wife had no right to inquire into the

conduct of her superior, whom she ought to presume to be chaste. She was expected to regard the evil manners and ill-treatment of her husband " as God's will and a cross which she must bear for the expiation of her sins," for the sin, in fact, of being a woman. " Our judgment," aptly quotes Pothier, " spares the raven and persecutes the dove." The legalisation of the husband's adultery, which reigned so long in Europe and still obtains in England, is the fruit of the Canon law. The wife was also expected to observe a purity before marriage which was not expected of her husband, and if at any time before marriage she had committed an indiscretion her husband could obtain a dissolution of the marriage on that ground, while if she committed adultery after marriage in order to escape from a tyrannical husband, she was compelled to remain married, for, being separated from her husband, she was condemned to live in adultery, and was not allowed to marry even after her husband's death if she had during his lifetime promised to marry another man. If she applied for a separation on account of her husband's cruelty he could always successfully plead that he was exercising his marital power of correcting her, even though he had nearly killed her, or though " witnesses heard her com-

78

plaining in her bed or saw her with livid eyes and
bandaged face." If she in any way retaliated or
defended herself she was also denied a remedy,
because she must "come to court with clean
hands." By the invention of the restitution
of conjugal rights she could always be compelled
to return to the authority of her husband. The
opinion of Jerome, which was relied upon by
the Canon lawyers, has been already given in a
previous chapter.*

Erasmus, a few years before Luther commenced his attack upon the Canon law, wrote
his "Colloquies," in which he gives us a picture
of the position of married women under the
Canon law. Two women were one day discussing their respective husbands. One of them,
who had been married for some years, denounced
her "good man" in the strongest terms for
wasting her dowry on drink, prostitutes and
gambling. She said that he had attempted to
lay hands on her on returning home from one of
his midnight orgies, but she had caught hold of
a stool and kept him at bay. She was determined that she would endure him no longer,
and said that she had made up her mind to
leave him, for she would rather live with a pig

* Rittershusius I, 1, and II, xxii ; Grat. Decret. 33, 2, 4 ; 11, 3, 3 ; 32,
6, 23 ; Pothier, *Mariage*, § 507 & foll ; Rittershusius II, viii ; Leyser,
§§ 315-6 ; Burn, p. 502 ; ch. ii, *supra* ; and Grat. Decret. 32, 7, 7.

than with a husband like hers. The other woman, who had only recently been married, held up her hands in horror at the idea of a woman venturing to do such a thing. By defaming her husband, she said, the wife defamed herself. It was not right for a woman to talk like that.

" Not right ? " replied the first woman. " If he does not treat me as his wife I shall certainly not look upon him as a husband."

" But Peter and Paul say that we must obey our husbands," said the young wife, " and even Sarah called her husband ' lord.' "

" Oh, yes, I've heard all that before," rejoined the other. " But Paul says that husbands should love their wives, and when he remembers his duty, I shall remember mine ; but not while he treats me as a servant."

" Whatever your husband is like," replied the young woman, in words which might have been taken from the " Decretals," " you ought to know that you have no right to change and get another. There used to be a remedy known as divorce, but now it has been abolished, and you will have to remain married to your husband to the end of your days."

" It must have been some infernal fiend who took away that right from us."

80

" Be careful what you say ! It was Christ who did it."

" I can hardly believe that."

" But so it was." *

The doctrine of the indissolubility of marriage, which was said to be laid down by the Gospel, clearly was never more than a Utopian idea, during the long reign of the Canon law, a rule which was never practised except to keep women in subjection and men and women under the perpetual tutelage of the Church. Men, and especially powerful or wealthy men, could always either obtain divorce or find some means of evading the rule even in the days when the Church was most powerful and had an opportunity of enforcing its doctrine. But litigation, especially where it concerned family troubles, was a perpetual source of profit to the Church, and, as Mr. Lea says, " was encouraged to the utmost to the infinite wretchedness of the people." All attempts to settle these differences out of court were repressed. Consent to a divorce or even to a separation was treated as collusion or fraud, and was sufficient to prevent the granting of any remedy unless the parties were wealthy or powerful, when their consent was encouraged. During the negotiations be-

* Erasmus, *Colloquia* (ed. 1719).

81

tween the Pope and Henry VIII of England about the divorce of Catherine of Aragon, every effort was made by the Papal lawyers to induce Catherine to consent to a divorce by taking a formal vow of chastity. The same King divorced Anne of Cleves with her consent, the ostensible ground being that the King had never " inwardly consented to the marriage, although it had been publicly and solemnly celebrated." The parties could, as we have seen, dissolve the marriage by consent where both retired to monasteries. For a long time, divorce on account of relationship could be obtained by what was practically mutual consent, for the mere confession of the parties was sufficient evidence. Pope Celestine III, however, condemned such evidence as collusion or fraud, and ordered that a scrupulous inquiry should be made into every case, and the scandal of the minutest public inquiry into the secrets of family life was perpetuated so that the Church might profit by this extensive litigation.

When the Canon law commenced its operations in Western Europe the Roman law and the Germanic, Frankish, Anglo-Saxon and other customs allowed divorce either by mutual consent or upon certain grounds where married life was intolerable or undesirable to either party, without in any case recourse having to be made to any tribunal. This system of divorce has always remained in force in Switzerland, in spite of the Canon law, although, owing to its influence, a public inquiry is now made into the reasons for the consent between the parties. The Canon law was always resisted by the people, wherever they had any voice in affairs, because of its interference with liberty and on account of its exactions. The jurisdiction of the bishops was always expressly excluded wherever liberty was retained by the people in the free towns and countries. The privileges of many of the free towns, such as Amsterdam, and the statutes of the various countries show that every effort was made by the people to oust the Canon law or restrict it in its operation. In many parts, down to the Reformation, the people had retained the right of going to their own locally elected judges and obtaining divorce either by mutual consent or on such grounds as desertion, adultery, long absence, or any act which was inconsistent with married life and the welfare of married people. From the thirteenth century onwards the people of Holland turned from the episcopal courts and opposed their sentences in spite of the Inquisition and the penances of the Church, while the people practically ignored the superior courts which followed the Canon law. The study of the Civil law in its original purity, without the glosses of the Canonists, assisted the popular movement and contributed in a great measure to the final overthrow of the Canon law. The Reformation was principally a popular movement against the Canon law, with its utter disregard for liberty and the welfare of the people and the morality of their lives. "Society," says Mr. Lea, "so long as it was orthodox and docile, was allowed to wallow in all the wickedness which depravity might suggest. The supreme object of uniformity of faith was practically attained and the moral condition of mankind was dismissed from consideration as of no importance." The condemnation of countless numbers of clergy and laity to enforced chastity could only lead, as it did lead, to adultery being pronounced by the Canon law to be a minor offence, although, or rather because, it was the principal ground for divorce by the same law. Concubinage was declared on the authority of one of the Popes to be no sin, while incest was almost the peculiar vice of the ecclesiastics, who had sole jurisdiction over divorce. "The world has probably never seen," says Mr. Lea, "a society more vile than that of

Europe in the fourteenth and fifteenth centuries." *

At the beginning of the sixteenth century, the end of what is known as the golden age of the Canon law, Europe was, as Erasmus tells us, "asphyxiated with formulas and human inventions. Nothing was heard of but dispensations, indulgences and the powers of the Pope." The law was made and administered by priests and monks, "who loved the life that now is," and consisted of vows, oaths and sacraments, which were usually no more than fictions or fetiches, and upon which the safety of the soul could in no measure be said to depend. "The Pharisees of this world will break the Sabbath for an ox or an ass, but will not relax an inch of their rule to save a perishing soul." Erasmus, when he ridiculed the Canon law of the indissolubility of marriage, knew from his own experience how a vow taken in early youth was used by the Church as an instrument of tyranny. "Shame on a law," he cries, "which says that a vow taken when the down is on the cheek is of perpetual obligation.

* Froude, *Life and Letters of Erasmus*, p. 376; Burn, *Eccles. Law*, p. 504; Burge (1910), III pp. 31 & 813; Pollock & Maitland II, vii, p. 390; Wessels, *Hist. of Roman-Dutch Law*, pp. 468-9; Stadboek van Amsterdam (privilege of 1332, etc.); Fockema Andreae's *Notes to Grotius*, V, 18; Blok, *Hist of the Netherlands*, I, p. 181 & *passim*; Lea, *Hist. of the Inquisition*, I, ch. i and III, ch. ix; Grat. Decret. 32, 7, 9-10.

A HISTORY OF DIVORCE

. . . What can a boy of seventeen brought up on books know of his mind ? '' A priest in a world where " celibates are many and the chaste few '' might be guilty of all manner of crime, but the only unpardonable sin for him was marriage. Exactly the same applied to divorce, especially in the case of a woman or one who could not obtain a dispensation or a divorce from the Pope. The monk who wished to discard his vow of chastity and marry was liable to be dragged back to his cell at any time, just as the wife, who discovered that she had made a mistake in her ignorance and extreme youth, was liable to be dragged back to the authority of a husband who could commit adultery and all kinds of crime with impunity. The choice of a woman in those days was usually that between enforced marriage and enforced celibacy, at a time when, as Mr. Lea says, " to take the veil was equivalent to becoming a public prostitute." *

There have been many commentaries upon the Canon law of divorce, but with the possible exception of Mr. Lea's *History of the Inquisition* probably the most illuminating of all is Machiavelli's *Prince*, which, appearing on the eve of

* Froude, *Life and Letters of Erasmus*, pp. 177-182, 312, etc ; Lea, *Hist. of the Inquisition (loc. cit.)*. See also p. 171 *infra*.

the Reformation and written by one who, like
Erasmus, died in the arms of the Catholic
Church, expresses its spirit and practice as no
other book can, based as it is upon the practice
of the princes and Popes of the Middle Ages.
Illustrating one of his well-known maxims, that
it is above all necessary " to play the hypocrite
well," especially in religion, and to be "neat
and cleanly " in one's collusions, he gives the
example (taken at random) of one Pope who was
one of the authors of the Canon law. Of him
he says that he " never did nor thought of anything but cheating, and never wanted matter
to work upon ; and though no man promised a
thing with greater asseveration nor confirmed it
with more oaths and imprecations, and observed
them less, yet understanding the world well
he never miscarried." Dante two centuries
before had placed Popes, such as Boniface VIII
and Clement V, who were responsible for some
of the principal rules of divorce, in his *Inferno*
and *Purgatorio*, together with innumerable
clerics who were " too obscure for any recognition," for " prostituting the things of God
for gold and silver." *

Such were the authors of the Canon law of

* Machiavelli's *Prince*, ch. xviii and *passim* ; Dante, *Inferno*, vii, 46-66,
xix ; *Purg.*, xix, 97 *ad fin.* ; xx, *esp.* 85-96.

divorce, and such were the principles and practice of that law which called itself the Law of Heaven (*jus poli*). It was laid down in times of ignorance, superstition, "force and fraud," in a time " of almost unrelieved blackness," when " the infliction of gratuitous evil was deemed the highest duty of man," and " the administration of law, both spiritual and secular, was little more than organised wrong and injustice," when " the wayward heart of man, groping in the twilight," often " under the best impulses, inflicted misery and despair on his fellow creatures, while thinking to serve God," and " the ambitious and unprincipled traded on those impulses to gratify the lust of avarice and domination." *

* Lea, *History of the Inquisition*, III, ch. ix ; *esp.* last two pages.

VI

THE REFORMATION

"The hour, the place and the man had met by a happy concurrence, and the era of modern civilisation and unfettered thought was opened, in spite of the fact that the Reformers were as rigid as the orthodox in setting bounds to dogmatic independence."

H. C. LEA, " A History of the Inquisition," III, p. 648.

IN 1517 Luther commenced the attack of the Reformation upon the Canon law in his *Babylonish Captivity of the Church*, in which he repudiated the sacramental conception and the indissolubility of marriage and affirmed that divorce was allowed by the Scriptures upon certain grounds. Three years later he gave expression to the feelings of more than half of Christendom by publicly burning the Canon law at Wittenburg, in the presence of a large gathering of doctors, students and citizens, with the memorable words, " Because thou hast vexed the Holy One of God, let the everlasting fire consume thee," and the students sang a Te Deum and a dirge over the ashes. " By this bold act," says his biographer, " Luther consummated his final rupture with

91

the papal system." The fire which Luther had
kindled quickly spread to other countries, and
within a few years Germany, Switzerland,
Holland, England, Scotland and the Scan-
dinavian countries had repudiated the authority
of the Canon law.*

Upon certain points the Reformers were all
agreed : that the Canon law was anti-Christian
and false law, that marriage was not a sacrament or spiritual matter, but a civil contract,
that judicial separation had no Scriptural authority, that divorce on the grounds of adultery
and malicious desertion was allowed by the
Scriptures, and that these grounds *ipso facto*
dissolved marriage without the necessity of a
judicial trial. Adultery as a ground for divorce
was based upon the same passages in St. Matthew
as the Canon lawyers had relied upon for their
doctrine of judicial separation. Malicious desertion was the peculiar invention of the Reformers
and was based upon the well-known text in St.
Paul (i Cor., 7, 15). These grounds for divorce
were, however, not in any way new, but represent what had been the practice in many parts
of Europe for centuries in spite of the Canon
law, and the Reformers, to strengthen their

---

* Köstlin. *Life of Luther*, ch. vii ; *Cambridge Modern History I,*
p. 136 and foll. ; Rittershusius, *pr.*

position were able to rely upon the practice of the Roman law and of the Canon law itself. It is not quite clear, in fact, whether, in formulating these grounds for divorce, the practice was made to square with the Scriptures, or the Scriptures were made to fit in with the practice. It is characteristic of the legal discussion of divorce for the next two or three centuries that the customs and wishes of the people were ignored as being irrelevant, while the Roman law, the authority of which was opposed by the Reformers to that of the Canon law, was rarely cited as an authority for the grounds for divorce, although, like the Canonists, the Reformers made its principles serve their dogma. The Scriptures, and the Scriptures alone, were regarded as the sole fountain of legislation in marriage, divorce and all other matters.

The first case dealing with malicious desertion in the Supreme Court of Holland illustrates the prevailing legal and theological views. This was a case in which the parties had been married in a neighbouring Catholic province at a time when both were Catholics, and the husband, afterwards becoming a Protestant and fearing the Inquisition, had fled to Holland and become a Dutch citizen, but his wife refused to follow him or to adopt the new religion. The husband appears to have done all he could to induce her to come to him in Holland, and to have assured her that he would in no way interfere with her in her religion. She, however, was unmoved by all this, and asserted that she was afraid that the children, who had remained with her, might be brought up in the Protestant faith if she came to Holland—a fear which was probably not ungrounded. She obtained a judicial separation from him on the ground of his heresy in the Court of the Archbishop in whose jurisdiction she resided, and finally wrote to her husband that she refused to return to him unless he returned to the Catholic faith, a resolution which she was " ready to sign with her blood." The husband thereupon applied to the Supreme Court of Holland for a divorce on the ground of her desertion. As she did not return after being summoned to do so, the court granted the divorce, gave the husband leave to marry again, and ordered the wife, who was declared to be a malicious deserter, to restore to him all the property which she had in her possession." *

In this case the Scriptural texts, the opinions of the Fathers and of the Reformed theologians were cited in court, together with the Roman

* 5 Holl. Cons., 46 and foll.

law doctrine of long absence. It is significant that the Canon law was also relied upon, and the reasoning of the Canon lawyers in interpreting the passage in St. Paul was fully adopted. The Canonists, as we have seen, had contended that the passage in St. Paul was sufficient to cover a case where one of the parties, owing to heresy or some other religious difference, had left the other, and that heresy was equivalent to idolatry, which was spiritual adultery. The Reformed lawyers and theologians, whose opinions were relied upon in this case, were not slow to make use of this argument and turn it against the Catholics, who, they contended, were heretics and even idolaters, and the husband could not therefore be expected to return to a spouse who was a Catholic, much less to the Catholic religion. The Scriptural text was, however, stretched even further than this. The spouses according to St. Paul owed each other the well-known " carnal debt," which the Canonists had also insisted upon. Therefore the wife, in this case, by refusing to pay this debt, and thus depriving her husband of the lawful means of escaping from unlawful desires, was guilty of a species of theft, robbing him, as one may say, of that which not enriched her and made him poor indeed. A deserter, it was said, was worse than an adulterer, for, according to Timothy, a man who deserted his wife and children was " worse than an infidel." The passage in Paul, it was contended, applied not only to cases where there was a religious fault on the part of one of them, but also every case in which either refused, from " any unjust or unlawful cause whatever," to fulfil his or her marital obligations. In such cases it was not the judge who separated those " whom God had joined," for the judge merely recognised that the separation had already taken place by the act of the deserting party, and he therefore could " with a clear conscience " confirm the divorce and grant leave to the innocent party to marry again, and the latter might, with an equally clear conscience, do so. The fact that it was the husband in this case who had left his wife, was overcome by the application of the Canonistic doctrine that the wife was bound to follow the husband wherever he chose to go, the domicil of the wife, according to the Roman law, being that of the husband. Such was the reasoning by which malicious desertion was legally established as a ground for divorce. Desertion and long absence had been long established as grounds for divorce in many parts of Europe, but it was the crowning achievement of the Reformers to treat it as "malicious" and make it into a crime. To go out of marriage, once being in, was a sort of crime, and so crime, and crime alone, was regarded by the Reformers, as it had been by the Canonists, as the only legal ground for divorce according to the Scriptures. We find Calvin citing the passage of the Canon law which says that "man does not separate those who are condemned for some crime," but in that case it is God, through the law, who separates.*

For more than two centuries divorce in Protestant countries remained in the hands of theologians, who alternately stretched or restricted the Scriptural texts to suit their doctrines. The Catholic Church, in answer to the Reformation, in the Council of Trent reasserted the Canon law, and although not laying down the indissolubility of marriage as a doctrine essential to salvation, formulated, for those who controverted this and other doctrines, more than "forty-nine distinct damnations." A long and bitter controversy raged between the Canonists and Jesuits on the one hand, of whom Bellarmine was the most celebrated and most subtle doctor, and the Reformers on the other,

---

* Grat. Decret. 33, 2, 18; Calvin, Lexicon, *s.v.* Divortium; 5 Holl. Cons. 46 and foll.

of whom Frederick Spanhemius, the Calvinist, was the principal and most ingenious exponent. The lawyers on both sides incorporated the opinions of their respective champions in their law-books, and the courts and legislatures made laws accordingly. Practical utility, and the wishes and welfare of the parties, were everywhere ignored. Only occasionally, and then merely as a subsidiary argument, do we find any attempt to make the Scriptures square with utility. Brouwer, for instance, one of the leading Dutch authorities of the middle of the seventeenth century, argues that a husband who deserts his wife and family is worse than an adulterer, because, while the latter is only carried away by the temporary allurements of strange women and usually returns to his wife and family, the former has not the same excuse, for he leaves his wife and family unprovided for. The doctrine of the " accidental adulteries " of the husband, which has had the authority of more than one English judge, was therefore not unknown to the Reformers, and the wife has always been expected to divinely forgive whenever her husband humanly errs. This argument of Brouwer's, however, is purely intended to support the Calvinistic view, for further on he holds that even where the parties are living under the same roof the one who refuses to pay the "carnal debt" is guilty of malicious desertion ; which is still good Roman-Dutch law. The Scriptures, in fact, remained the divine fountain of the divorce law, and we find Voet as late as the end of the seventeenth century saying that " by modern usage agreeing with the divine law, there are only two just grounds for dissolving the marriage tie, viz., adultery and malicious desertion," and citing the Scriptural texts and the writings of the Reformed theologians, especially Spanhemius, in support of this. The Scriptural texts were positive laws which it was the duty of legislators and judges to observe and enforce, and all other considerations were ignored.*

The Canonistic interpretations of these texts were alternately refuted and adopted by the Reformers. The sacramental aspect of marriage, the idea of the unity of flesh involved in that conception, the condemnation of innocent and guilty alike to celibacy, were all controverted at great length, and those Scriptural texts alone were considered to be applicable to divorce which were interpreted to mean that crime was the only justification for di-

* Brouwer II, ch. xxii ; J. Voet ad Pandectas 24, 2, 5–9 ; Groenewegen ad Cod. 5, 17.

vorce. The wonder is that where they discarded so much they thought it necessary to attempt to follow the Scriptures at all. But the age was theological, and the Reformers had in the Jesuits the keenest of competitors, who would have been only too glad of an opportunity of branding them as atheists. The Reformers insisted upon the secular and political as opposed to the ecclesiastical aspect of marriage. Marriage did not, they affirmed, belong to divine as opposed to human law, " for it embraces nothing which concerns faith, eternal salvation, Church discipline or Church administration." The public ceremony before a marriage officer, who might be either a magistrate or a clergyman, was considered to be evidence of the essentially secular character of marriage. Divorce, similarly, only required the sanction of the judge or of the sovereign. But the general trend of legal discussion being theological, persistent attempts were made by the lawyers and divines to adapt the texts of the Scriptures to this conception of marriage. The public ceremony of marriage, instead of being treated, as it was intended to be, as the best evidence of marriage—to put an end to secret marriages— we find the lawyers and theologians—though some of them admit that marriage is really a private contract as in the Roman law—saying that it is really God who joins the parties through the sovereign or magistrate, who is His earthly representative according to St. Paul. The same authority, therefore, and that authority alone, can separate those " whom God hath joined " in this public manner. They did not see that once it is admitted that man, whether that man be sovereign, judge or pope, can separate the parties there is no reason why the parties themselves, who, according to modern notions, are represented by judges and sovereigns in judicial and legislative functions, should not themselves be allowed to separate. This, as we have seen, was practically recognised in the case of desertion, where it was held that the judge merely confirmed a separation which had already taken place. But the Reformers, like the Canonists, would not give up a contentious jurisdiction which was a source at once of profit and of power. The spiritual courts, which they had universally condemned, were practically continued in many countries under the new *régime*, and even where all the judges, as in Holland, or some of the judges, as in Germany and Scotland, were secular, the hold of the theologians over the practice of the Courts was jealously maintained, and any attempt to depart from the strict letter of the Scriptures was condemned as heretical. Leyser, one of the most eminent consistorial judges of Saxony, was persecuted for the breadth of his views. The destruction of the Canon law by Luther and Zwingli was followed by the construction of the new law and system of judicial practice. It is in the ecclesiastical ordinances of Geneva, and the practice of that consistorial court, which are to be found in the writings of Beza, Calvin's biographer and right-hand man, that the substantive law and judicial practice of the Reformation really originated. Calvin and Beza may be said to be the jurists of the Reformation. The practice of Geneva, which was established by the middle of the sixteenth century, became the pattern of judicial practice, and, sooner or later, was followed in all the Protestant countries with the sole exception of England, which, for reasons which will be examined in a later chapter, adopted a peculiar procedure of its own. Divorce, in all these countries, on any other ground than adultery or malicious desertion, was forbidden, and it was laid down by the Church as advice to the judges that it was their duty to attempt in every possible way to reconcile the parties, an idea which is clearly a continuation of the episcopal functions. The extraordinary discretion which the judge was allowed to exercise, with a view mainly to the prevention of divorce where there was any agreement between the parties or any assistance had been given by either to the other to obtain a divorce, is another instance of the continuation of the episcopal judge. The will and welfare of the parties were treated as irrelevant. The Canonistic doctrines of collusion, connivance and recrimination were fully adopted, and divorce was made as difficult as possible in spite of its divine origin. Private separations were reprobated and punished. In Amsterdam, for instance, married persons who lived apart without judicial authority were fined a hundred florins for this crime (*flagitium*) for every month while such separation lasted, and the payment of the fine was enforced by imprisonment. If one party was unwilling to renew cohabitation, the other had an action for the restitution of conjugal rights, and if such rights were not restored, the defaulting party was liable to be condemned and divorced as a malicious deserter. Brouwer says that judges should not easily grant either divorces or separations because " the anger of lovers is wont to lead to the renewal of love," and he fears that there may be scandal to Church and State and that

103

the propagation of members for both will be in danger, besides which spouses who live separately and " remain idle " are subject to the wiles of Satan. The writings of the Reformation period are filled with references to " the gift of chastity " and to the parties " burning in the flames of concupiscence," but with the exception of a " hope of reconciliation," which in most cases was, as Brouwer calls it, " uncertain," and which was used as a fiction to force the parties to live together against their wills, there is never a reference in all this to affection between the parties being in any way necessary to marriage. Marriage was, according to this view, no more than political machinery invented principally for the avoidance or rather the concentration of sexual weakness, and the parties, once they had entered into it, were made to outwardly conform to an iron rule, which was said to be based upon Christ's teaching, which was dissolved with the greatest difficulty and never without public disgrace, while any unauthorised cessation from matrimonial duties, even where the parties realised that they were unable to live together and were willing to release one another, was punished as a crime and regarded as a sin.*

* Brouwer I, 9, and II, ch. xxix and *cap. ult.* ; Stadboek of Amsterdam (ordinance of 1586) ; Rittershusius II, viii.

The whole conception of divorce as established by the Reformation may be conveniently summarised in the definition of Brouwer, who calls it " the violent dissolution of a marriage, made by the authority of a judge with the intention of constituting a perpetual division and after an inquiry into the cause of the divorce." This definition shows the confusion of ideas which prevailed among the Reformers, who endeavoured to reconcile their own interpretations of the Scriptures as far as possible with the Canon and Roman laws. The intention of effecting a final separation is taken from the Roman law, but in that law the intention was that of the parties themselves, which the Reformers rejected as strenuously as the Canonists had done. The parties could have no intention in the matter, or if they had any it was unlawful and even sinful. The word " violent," which is typical of all the laws of divorce which have had their origin in ecclesiastical laws, was used by Brouwer, as he tells us, to express the fact that the separation was made without the consent of the parties. The judge or magistrate was said to represent God in the matter, just as the papal lawyers had held that the Pope or bishop represented the Deity. The judge was, in other words, the legal successor of the bishop, and his court a continuation of that spiritual jurisdiction which combined the confessional and the Inquisition. A public inquiry into the causes of divorce was therefore essential, and as the only grounds for divorce were adultery and desertion, this trial took the form of a private prosecution of one spouse by the other, in which the plaintiff had to prove his own innocence and the guilt of the defendant, and had to undergo the most searching cross-examination at the hands of a judge, whose duty was to keep the parties married in outward form as long as possible, before they could obtain a divorce. The dispensing power which had been in the hands of the Popes was retained by the prince or parliament, and still remains in some form or other in many modern Protestant countries.*

The Canon law, having made adultery the fundamental ground for divorce, had quite logically come to treat it as a minor offence. The Reformation, however, was in many respects a moral revolt against the immoralities for which a system which outwardly enforced celibacy was held to be responsible, and the Reformers entered upon a severe and minute crusade against immorality. The writings of the Reformed theologians and lawyers are full of dis-

* Brouwer, *ubi supra*, and II, *cap. ult.* ; Groenewegen, ad Cod, 5, 17.

sertations and condemnations of prostitution and concubinage, which had been connived at and even made lawful. All these institutions, which were the natural accompaniments of a rigid law of divorce, were condemned by statute and severely punished, at any rate so far as the woman was concerned. Adultery and malicious desertion, which were now made the only legitimate outlets from marriage, were punished by fine, imprisonment, forfeiture and banishment, and it is the common complaint among lawyers of this period that adultery was not made into a capital crime. They overlooked the fact, however, that while adultery in the Roman law was a capital crime, in theory at least it must have been a rare offence, as the parties by that law were not bound to retain a legal form of marriage when all affection between the parties had ceased to exist. There was therefore no excuse for adultery in the Roman law. But a prescription making adultery the principal cause of divorce had grown under the Canon law. For about a century after the Reformation in most Protestant countries adultery remained the sole legal ground for divorce in judicial practice, and it followed of necessity that adultery must be committed where the spouses were unable or unwilling to live together and one or both wished to marry again, and it was the acme of dogmatism to punish those who made use of the only legal exit. The choice of the parties was therefore between two prisons, that of an unhappy or intolerable marriage and that of a public gaol, and the Reformers could not long expect to compel those who made their escape from the one to enter the other. When desertion was afterwards established in judicial practice as a ground for divorce the Reformers, true to their essential idea that crime alone was a ground for divorce, called it " malicious " and turned it into a crime with the same penalties as for adultery, though they could find no Biblical authority for its punishment. Some of these penalties were often evaded or anticipated by one of the spouses going into voluntary and perpetual exile. Leyser, an eminent German authority, who for a long time was the presiding judge over the consistorial court at Wittenburg, writing in the middle of the eighteenth century, says that no mortal evil is so dangerous as that which daily pleases Venus to unite unequal forms and souls in the iron yoke of marriage, and that the so-called indissoluble bond of marriage, which is said to bind for ever persons who differ in their whole minds and characters, has been the cause of more banishments than the criminal laws of Charles V, has dissipated more property than theft and robbery, and has rendered more citizens unfit for fulfilling their duties as citizens than luxury itself.*

But the divorce laws of the Reformation, though in some respects made equivalent to criminal laws by statute, were largely made by judges and jurists. The influence of the jurists in making the laws during the Reformation period cannot be exaggerated. This was done under the pretext that the writings of the jurists were taken as evidence of custom, and as the jurists followed the traditions of the Canon law a great deal of that law was gradually incorporated into legal practice. As we have seen, the customs of the people had everywhere, before the Reformation, rejected the Canon law, but now the people, who were crushed at an early stage, were obliged to conform to the new laws and the doctrine of the divine right of kings, and, by one of the most stupendous instances of judge-made or jurist-made law known in history,

---

* Leyser, *Meditationes ad Pandectas*, vol. V, *spec.* 290 ; Brouwer II, *cap. ult.* A Dutch law of the 1st of April, 1580, says that adultery is indulged in with impunity because the magistrates, "in adjudging such misusages and crimes, consider them of very little moment." (*Laws of British Guiana*, vol. II, App. A.).

the Canon law was incorporated into legal practice, almost in its entirety, under the guise of its being customary law. The Reformers themselves had called the Canon law anti-Christian, and Luther had expressed the feeling of the majority of the people when he burnt it at Wittenburg. But its ashes were gradually revived by the Reformed jurists and theologians, who in their attempt to build up a new divine law and practice found in the Canon law a ready-made machinery which they adapted to their own use. The use which the Reformers made of the Canon law surpasses that which the Canonists had made of the Roman law, and to complete the irony of it, the Reformers continued to see the Roman law through the eyes of the Canonists. In some countries the new statutory law, while condemning the guilty party to some secular penalty, said nothing about the right to re-marry, which was expressly laid down only so far as the innocent party was concerned. The right of the guilty party to re-marry, and even the question whether the marriage was legally dissolved at all, was only settled by judicial decision after a long controversy in which the Canon law was largely drawn upon. For a long time the practice prevailed that the guilty party was not allowed to marry until the death or re-marriage

110

of the innocent party. Van Leeuwen, writing in the middle of the seventeenth century, says that even after divorce, " so long as the deserted party lives single and some hope of reconciliation remains, the marriage bond can by no means be said to be severed." This restriction against the re-marriage of the guilty party was maintained because it was thought that by allowing such re-marriage the guilty party would profit by his own crime. It was only gradually that this restriction was removed by judicial decision, and after it had been pointed out by more than one eminent authority, including Bynkershoek, in the middle of the eighteenth century, that a divorce which dissolved the marriage and left one party still bound was an absurdity.*

The jurists and theologians also maintained that where one party had been guilty of adultery, the intermarriage between the adulterers should not be allowed for the same reasons. This restriction also was borrowed from the Canon law. After a long controversy as to whether it was necessary in such a case for the adulterer to have made a promise to marry his or her accomplice, or to have made an attempt upon the

* Brouwer II, *cap. ult.* and *passim* ; Van Zijl, Judicial Practice of South Africa, 2nd ed., pp. 482-3 ; Rittershusius II, 8 ; Van Leeuwen, Censura Forensis, 1, 1, 15, 14 ; Bynkershoek, Jur. Priv., II. 8-10 and 18.

life of the other spouse as in the Canon law, all intermarriages between adulterers were at last in some countries by statute expressly forbidden. This restriction still remains in most Protestant countries, except where it has more recently, as in Germany and England, been abolished by statute.

The adoption of these Canonistic restrictions which condemned one party to celibacy, either perpetually or as regards some particular person, is only one of many instances in which the practice of the Reformers was utterly at variance with their previous condemnation of enforced celibacy. But a more glaring contradiction followed. The Reformers had above all condemned the Canonistic separation from bed and board, and the enforced celibacy to which it relegated the parties. This was regarded by them as being directly opposed to the Apostolic injunction that marriage was the divinely appointed refuge for those who had not the " gift of chastity." The punishment of the innocent party by this means was especially condemned. But we find the lawyers even a century after the Reformation, while censuring this institution, going on to defend and actually to adopt it in a large and growing number of cases. Judicial separation was adopted to cover causes of divorce

112

which did not fit in with the Scriptural grounds of adultery and malicious desertion. Brouwer says that it is allowed on any of the Roman law grounds for divorce or where there is " excessive cruelty or unspeakable crime." He will not allow divorce in such cases because the Scriptures do not sanction it, and because he considers that there is still a " hope of reconciliation," however " uncertain." As the Scriptural texts were treated as positive laws, judicial separation came to be applied as a compromise for all those serious causes which had been grounds for divorce under the Roman law, and afterwards for all cases in which the parties agreed to a judicial separation so long as the judge after public inquiry was satisfied that a sufficient ground for the separation existed. The mere agreement between the parties, however, was not sufficient, and judges refused to sanction separations unless there were at least continual quarrels between the parties. The origin of this adoption of judicial separation by the Reformers may best be told in the words of Bynkershoek.*

Bynkershoek reviews the history of the Roman and Canon laws of divorce, saying that by the Canon law marriage had been called a sacrament,

* Brouwer, II, 29 ; Groenewegen ad Cod. 5, 17; Bynkershoek Jur. Priv. II, 8.

113

and therefore there appeared to the Canonists no sufficiently suitable ground for dissolving it. To meet the difficulties which this opinion encountered in practice, certain grounds for divorce were invented of which the most notable was impotence, " an egregious ground worthy of the dignity of a sacrament " ! He then goes on to say that the Reformers abolished the sacramental conception of marriage, together with many other superstitions, but they still thought that there was something divine in marriage, so they also made its dissolution difficult, and, instead of following the Roman law, relied upon other Scriptural authorities which, they contended, defined adultery and malicious desertion as the sole grounds for divorce. But seeing that this opinion also was not without its difficulties in practice, they began to make malicious desertion as mild as possible and extended it as far as they could. They also made use of another remedy which had been in frequent use in the Canon law, and which they adopted, as nothing better was forthcoming. They saw that there were, among the grounds for divorce in the Roman law, some which, if we love truth, were even more serious than adultery and malicious desertion, for what husband would not prefer the unchastity or desertion of his wife to an attempt by her upon his life ?—which was a most just ground for divorce in that law. They saw all this, and, in order to extricate themselves from their difficulty, where there were grounds in practice as grave as or even graver than adultery and malicious desertion, they adopted as a general remedy the Canonistic separation from bed and board, which was unknown to the Romans, and invented to meet necessity by the Canonists, so that spouses, who could only be divorced on the grounds mentioned, should be prevented from injuring or even killing each other in their anger. The grounds for this separation were not easy to define, being left to the discretion of the judge, who had to satisfy himself that a suitable ground existed, whether the parties agreed to it or not, with the hope that they would at some time become reconciled. So the bonds and the empty name of marriage remained, but in order that the bodies of the parties might not harm one another, the parties were separated, and it was not the business of the judge to ascertain whether they had the gift of chastity or not, or sought satisfaction elsewhere, or were ever likely to become reconciled again. Judicial separation was frequently made use of in Holland by many who were unable to obtain divorces, and was rarely, if ever, followed by reconciliation between the parties.*

So it came about that within less than a century of the Reformation the Reformers, who had condemned the Canon law as anti-Christian and even treasonable, followed it in all matrimonial causes in preference to the Roman law. Bynkershoek condemns Brouwer and the rest of the jurists, who, as he says, were almost suffocated by the foulness of the Canon law till they could scarcely breathe, and, while not denying the authority of the Canon law, he says that we must be careful that its authority does not become greater than it ought to be. The Canon law, indeed, after being exorcised, expelled and even burnt, returned, like the famous unclean spirit, and found its abode empty, swept and garnished, and, taking other choice spirits more evil than itself, entered and dwelt there, and " the last state of that man was worse than the first." The new wine of the Reformation was poured into the old bottles and mixed with the lees of the old wine.†

The bibliolatry of the Reformers and their " helpless dependence on the letter of Scripture "

---

* Bynkershoek, *Jur. Priv.* II, 8.

† Bynkershoek, *loc. cit.* ; Rittershusius, pr. and II, 10 ; Van Leeuwen, Cens. For. 1, 1, 1, 20.

led them, like the Papal lawyers before them, into "consequences subversive of Christian morality." Polygamy, which St. Augustine was unable to condemn, and which the Popes had allowed because the Bible had not condemned it, notably in the case of Henry IV of Castile, was even advocated in preference to divorce by Luther and some of the leading Reformers, not only in the well-known case of Philip of Hesse, but in that of Henry VIII of England. When Henry was seeking Scriptural sanction for that divorce, " the ultimate solution of which," as Lord Acton says, " was the separation of England from the Church," the opinions of Luther, Melancthon and Bucer, among many others, were obtained. These divines responded that what had been done by the patriarchs of old could not be forbidden, and therefore it was not unlawful that a man should have more wives than one at the same time. The King, they argued, would be justified by human law in divorcing Catherine, but they did not wish to recommend divorce in his case, because it was not allowed by the Scriptures, and was therefore a sin. Although the authority of the divine law was liable to be exaggerated, they preferred to exaggerate, if necessary, the authority of the magistrate in all political matters, for many things were permitted to a magistrate which in the case of other people might be called in question. For reasons of State, therefore, and in order that the King might follow the dictates of his conscience, they advised him, not to divorce Catherine, but to take an additional wife, for by so doing his action could not injure or insult the conscience or reputation of anyone, including his present Queen. Polycarpus Leyser, an eminent Protestant theologian and judge at Dresden, disallowed divorce in a certain case on the ground of leprosy, but told the husband that if he could not conquer his desires he was justified in consulting his conscience and satisfying himself in other ways if so advised. This preference of immorality and polygamy to divorce is only the logical result of all attempts to dogmatise in the matter of divorce.*

The position of married women was not greatly modified in practice by the Reformation. Men and women alike being compelled to conform to rigid Scriptural rules, regardless of their wishes or welfare, women, whose legal and economic position was as a rule inferior to that of men, suffered more than men under the new *régime.*

* Acton, *The History of Freedom*, pp. 159-160, and notes, where the texts of the opinions of Luther, etc., are given in the original ; Köstlin, *Life of Luther*, pp. 429-432 ; Leyser, V. *spec.* 315.

THE REFORMATION

By the Reformation all men and women had been declared to be their own priests, but this opinion, like the promises of reformers in all times, was never observed in practice when the new laws had established themselves. Technically, husband and wife had equal rights over each other's bodies, as St. Paul had said, and as the lawyers laid down. But in most countries the wife was expected to endure with patience the cruelty, adulteries and other misconduct of her husband, who was still regarded as her " head." The wife was legally a minor and had no legal personality or any right to the children, whom she had borne, until the death of her husband or until she sued him for a divorce or a separation. The metaphor of the Canon law that the husband is the soul and the wife the body was used by Brouwer to express the essential difference between the rights of husband and wife. The property which the husband had in the wife and her legal subjection to him appeared to have the sanction of both divine and natural laws. Except in the cases where the wife was a public trader, all her earnings after marriage were presumed to have been obtained either by adultery or by theft from her husband. The husband had the sole right of disposal even of her separate property, and she could not interdict him from wasting it in debauchery without the expense and disgrace of a public trial, and often when it was too late. The fiction that the domicil of the wife was that of her husband was borrowed from the Canon law and applied to divorce, so that a wife could not obtain a divorce unless she followed her husband wherever he chose to go, and if she did not follow him she was liable to be divorced and punished as a malicious deserter. The husband was not allowed to divest himself of his marital power by any legal means. If the husband had been absent for many years and had left the wife unprovided for, she was not allowed to marry again unless she could prove that his absence was malicious, while if she married again she was, besides being liable to prosecution for bigamy, bound to return to his authority if he returned and chose to accept her. Bynkershoek in such a case coolly compares the wife to a horse which has been used by other men, and says that while a man would take the horse he could not be expected to accept a wife who had been used even by his friends.* The action for damages which the husband had for his wife's adultery, which was regarded as an offence against the husband, is another instance

* *Jur. Priv.* II, 16, 9.

of the property which the husband had in his wife. As under the Canon law, the wife had practically no protection against her husband's ill-treatment, for the right of chastisement was maintained in all its vigour. Brouwer in advocating the more humane treatment of wives is compelled to rely upon Pagan writers, such as Cato and Marcus Aurelius, for a law which Christianity did not appear to allow. If the wife left her husband on account of his cruelty she was refused the remedy of divorce, and was compelled to return to his authority if he gave security for good behaviour, and if she did not do so she was liable to all the penalties of divorce as a malicious deserter, including the loss of a portion of her property and, what was the most important in her eyes, of the custody of her children. Public opinion always condemned the wife, and where she was unhappily married made her choice one between slavery and the stigma of being a divorced or separated woman, for public opinion then, as now, always excused the man and condemned the woman, no matter what the merits of the case might be. The laws which the monks had laid down before the Reformation continued in force, and the position of women was in many respects worse than it had been under the Canon law, for the refuge of the cloister was taken away. The laws continued to be written and expounded in a learned language, which as a rule she was not allowed to learn, and this fact alone is sufficient to account for the frivolous and insulting language relating to women employed by the most celebrated jurists.*

The effect of the Reformation upon the Canon law of divorce has been seen to have been very slight. Dogma succeeded dogma, and the divine right of kings under the influence of Reformed ministers was substituted for that of the Popes. All that the Reformation achieved was, by splitting up the power of the Churches and making religious toleration possible at a future time, gradually to secularise marriage and divorce. The insistence of the Reformers upon the secular and contractual nature of marriage assisted in the process. But for more than three centuries after the Reformation— and to a great extent to this day—old and new dogma ruled side by side in neighbouring countries, and people were compelled to obey a divine law which varied according to the view of it which was incorporated in the laws of the

---

* Grotius. Intro. I, 5, 1 and 18-27; *Rights of Peace and War*, II, 5, 9 and 11 ; Brouwer, II, 28 and 29 and *cap. ult.* ; Burge, 2nd Ed., III, 359 and foll. ; Kersterman, Woordenboek, s.v., Dissolutie ; Zurck, Codex Batavus, *s.v.*, Houwelijk ; Voet, 23, 2, 52 ; Leyser, §§, 290 and 313.

land. Married persons who had been capable of entering into marriage, when they discovered later that they were utterly unsuited to one another, were treated as children who were incapable of consenting to a divorce, and were compelled to prosecute one another in a public court with a vindictiveness which, if they did not feel, they were obliged to dissemble before they could obtain even a separation from each other. Divorce, which could only be obtained through crime and disgrace, was treated as itself criminal and disgraceful in all cases, and this tradition is still firmly embedded in law and public opinion. Clerical tutelage and the Inquisition and confessional, which the Reformers had aimed at overthrowing, remained in force. "When the last of the Reformers died," says Lord Acton, "religion, instead of emancipating the nations, had become an excuse for the criminal art of despots. Calvin preached, and Bellarmine lectured, but Machiavelli reigned." *

* Acton, *History and Freedom*, p. 44.

123

VII

FROM THE REFORMATION TO THE FRENCH REVOLUTION

Whoso prefers matrimony or other ordinance before the good of man and the plain exigence of charity, let him profess Papist, or Protestant, or what he will, he is no better than a Pharisee, and understands not the Gospel.

MILTON.

IT was soon found that the rigid laws which the Reformers had made could no more be maintained in practice than the Canon law had been. Until the French Revolution the story of divorce is that of the gradual interpretation and extension of these laws to meet the exigencies of practical life, and the development of a strong movement in favour of discarding all attempts to base the law of divorce upon any interpretation of particular Scriptural texts. The Reformation had been brought about, as we have seen, by an almost universal feeling of discontent with the Canon law, on the part of the people and of their rulers and teachers. The people, who had hailed Luther as the champion of liberty, which had been promised to every Christian man and woman, were soon crushed by both rulers and ecclesiastics, and discovered that they had only changed masters, and had become mere material upon which the new interpretations of the Scriptures were practised. The voice of the people, once the Reformation had been established, was silenced, and was not heard again for nearly three centuries, when it appeared in the thunder of the French Revolution. The researches and criticisms of humanists, who had studied the Roman law and the history of pre-papal times, had been made use of by the Reformers in bringing about the Reformation. Once the Reformation was complete, the Reformers continued to make use of this learning to strengthen their own dogma. But both before and after the Reformation there were a few eminent thinkers who saw that it was impossible to base the law of divorce upon the Scriptures. It is to these, who included in their number jurists, judges, statesmen and even ecclesiastics, that we must look mainly for the source of the interpretations and extensions of the laws which actually were made, and for the gradual movement towards, and the fore-shadowing of, the separation between law and theology and between Church and State. Some of those advocated the adoption of the Roman law or similar principles, some maintained that the spirit rather than the letter of Christianity should be followed, while others preferred to follow the Law of Nature, based upon the reason and experience of mankind, a conception which owes its origin principally to the Roman law.

A few years before the publication of Luther's *Babylonish Captivity*, Sir Thomas More, who, like Erasmus, whose friend he was, died a Catholic, wrote his *Utopia.* Of More, who afterwards became Lord Chancellor of England, Lord Acton says that he was one of the first Christian writers who " did not make his politics subservient to either Pope or King." More had in view the abolition of defects which existed in the English laws of that day, and in order to exclude all attempts to base the laws which he proposed upon the Scriptures, he found it advisable to imagine a country in which not Christianity but religious toleration and the will of the people were the foundation of the laws. He urges, for almost the first time in history since the Christian Emperors of Rome, the advisability of allowing divorce by mutual consent as well as in cases where one of the parties was guilty of adultery or " intolerable wayward manners." " Whereas," he says, " the man and the woman cannot well agree between themselves, both of them finding other, with whom they hope to live more quietly and merrily," they, " with the full consent of them both are divorced asunder and married again to other." This divorce is granted by leave of the council —for there are no lawyers in Utopia—who, " with their wives, diligently try and examine the matter." The author of this view of divorce was one of the most saintly and domestic as well as one of the most learned men of his time, a time when marriage was technically indissoluble, and when, as a contemporary authority says, the absence of domestic affection and the prevalence of licentiousness were amazing; when, though there was scarcely a man in love, and " Englishmen kept guard over their wives, offences against married life could always among them in the end be condoned for money." As Shakespeare makes Shylock say :

" These be the Christian husbands ! I have a daughter ;
Would any of the stock of Barabbas
Had been her husband rather than a Christian !" *

A few years later Cranmer, Latimer and other English bishops, lawyers and laymen advocated

* More's *Utopia* ; *Cambridge Modern History*, II, p. 492 ; *Merchant of Venice*, IV, i, 296.

similar views when they proposed to allow divorce in the ecclesiastical courts whenever there was deadly enmity between the parties.* About a century later, Milton, who called himself " the sole advocate of a discountenanced truth," wrote his *Doctrine and Discipline of Divorce*, and pointed out that divorce by mutual consent or at the will of either party without the necessity of a judicial inquiry into the causes of the divorce, was not inconsistent with the spirit of Christianity. He showed that the indissolubility of marriage and the trial of divorce cases were purely Papal inventions for temporal power and had no warrant in the Gospels. It was the spirit of Christianity, which was charity, that ought to be followed rather than any particular texts of the Scriptures. He condemned the application of those texts to the law by Catholics and Protestants alike. " Our Saviour's words touching divorce," he says, " are congealed into a strong rigour inconsistent both with His doctrine and His office, and that which He preached only to the conscience is by commercial tyranny snatched into a compulsive censure of a judicial court." No court was capable of inquiring into " the secret reason of dissatisfaction between man and wife."

* See chapter IX, *infra.* pp. 175-6.

131

To inquire into these causes and to " bandy up and down " their sufferings by means of " hired masters of tongue-fence," was to unnecessarily aggravate the sufferings of the parties. A judicial inquiry was only necessary when some question of property arose about which the parties could not agree. Marriage was based upon affection, and was intended rather " for the mutual enjoyment of that which the wanting soul needfully seeks than of that which the plenteous body would joyfully give away." The " burning " of which the apostle spoke remained and was even intensified where the parties through no fault of their own hated each other and " mourned to be separated." To enforce rigid adherence to an outward bond which existed in name was to encourage hypocrisy and to intensify the hatred of the parties, who even longed for each other's death. It was useless to attempt to strive to " glue an error together " which God and Nature would not join. There could be no harm to either party, while marriage would gain in honour, when both were able to obtain a divorce where affection had ceased to exist. " Our Saviour," he says, " was never more grieved and troubled than to meet with such a peevish madness among men against their own freedom." " Be not righteous overmuch," he says in effect. The Parliament to which Milton appealed was, however, too busily engaged in disputing " the divine right of kings " with Charles I to legislate in a matter of this kind, and nothing was done.*

Selden, Milton's great contemporary, whose motto was " Above all things, Liberty," made deep researches into the Hebrew laws of divorce, which are now little known, but which for centuries to come were made use of by Continental jurists. " Of all actions of a man's life," said he who had cause to know it, " his marriage does least concern other people, yet of all actions of our life 'tis the most meddled with by other people." Selden, a keen critic of the ecclesiastical laws, showed in his *Hebrew Wife* that Moses had not defined the grounds for divorce, but had laid down the necessity of the sending of a bill of divorce and had indicated only one of many grounds upon which a husband or wife might divorce each other. The words in Deuteronomy had been the subject of a dispute at the time of Christ between two schools of lawyers. The school of Schammai held that the words meant that there must be some disgraceful or criminal act, while that of Hillel contended that they meant that a man might divorce his wife for any

* Milton, *The Doctrine and Discipline of Divorce*, and *Tetrachordon*.

cause whatever, such as if she were unpleasing to him. The Greek word for " fornication " in the passage in St. Matthew was a general term including not only adultery, but any disgraceful or criminal act whatever. Christ had condemned both schools by referring marriage and divorce, like all other matters, to first principles, and above all to the principle of charity, which did not justify a husband in divorcing his wife either at will or even where she had been guilty of some disgraceful conduct.*

Grotius, who suffered for the broadness of his religious views by exile, at first held that adultery was the only Scriptural ground for divorce, but in his Notes on St. Matthew he accepted the view of Selden, and said that adultery was only one of many acts which were inconsistent with the existence of the marriage tie. The intention of Christ appeared to be to show how, by this most striking example, a good man might make use of the civil law of divorce without injury to his wife, to his own conscience or to anyone. There were many other reasons for irreconcilable hatred besides adultery, such as an attempt by the one upon the life of the other. Marriage was intended, not only for the begetting of children,

* Selden, *Uxor Ebraica*, 3, 22-31, cited in Brouwer, II, 18 and 23 ; Leyser, *Meditationes ad Pandectas*, *spec.* 313, corollary B. Voorda, Theses ; Gibbon, ch. xliv ; Pufendorf VI. i. 23.

but for the mutual assistance which was expected of the union. The question was whether the conduct of the one spouse was supportable to the other, and "perhaps our Saviour had this distinction in view." A man who married a woman who had been lawfully divorced was not only not guilty of adultery, but was even to be commended for saving her from possible degradation. Christ had not laid down the necessity of a judicial inquiry into the causes of divorce, and by the Hebrew and Roman laws of that time no such trial was necessary. He had neither designed to abolish the existing laws of divorce nor to make any positive laws upon the subject at all, but had merely laid down precepts for the guidance of the conscience of the individual, just as He had said that we ought to love our enemies. Charity, above all, was the perfection and essential principle of the Gospel, and that included what was for the benefit of both parties.*

In 1670 Pufendorf discussed the question of divorce solely from the point of view of the so-called Law of Nature. He inquires whether marriage, which is a contract of natural law,

---

* Grotius, *Annotationes ad Matthaeum*, 5, 32, cited by Barbeyrac in Grotius' *Rights of Peace and War* (London, 1738), II, 5, 9; B. Voorda, *Theses* (on *Dig.*, 24, 2).

is indissoluble, or whether divorce is allowable, a question which, he says, has been discussed with a great deal of heat. The object of marriage being the begetting of children and the mutual use of each other's bodies by the spouses, by the law of nature adultery and desertion, *i.e.*, an obstinate refusal on the part of either to perform the marital duties, are breaches of the contract entitling the offended party to dissolve it. He does not agree with the Roman conception of marriage as a partnership based on consent and dissoluble either by consent or at the will of either party, but regards it as a sort of natural and physical slavery which has something sacred in it, and which for reasons of public policy should be dissolved only for very weighty causes. He condemns the Canon Law and says that ecclesiastics always found a means of evading their own doctrine when they wished to favour any particular person, by showing that the marriage had never existed at all. The indissolubility of marriage was solely due to the Inquisition and the tyranny of the Popes. One of the reasons given by the sacred writers for exhorting people to marry was in order that they might avoid temptation, but a man who was perpetually chagrined by his wife was subject to greater temptation than ever. He cites an ancient Hebrew writer who says that nothing is more useful to marriage than the right of divorce, which is likely to keep both parties agreeable to each other and to maintain the peace of the family.*

Leyser, who died in 1752, was an eminent German jurist, who for many years presided over the Consistorial Court at Wittenburg, in Saxony, and was persecuted for his avowed dislike to all dogma. His views on divorce are á sort of compromise between the views of Pufendorf and those of the Reformers. As the Roman law of divorce was not considered to be applicable, he finds it necessary to make use of the law of nature in order to make the laws of the Reformers, which he was bound to administer, more suitable to the needs of the human beings who applied to him for divorces. He shows the absurdity of the prevalent custom of relying upon the Canon law to support the laws made by the Reformers. The objects of marriage, he says, are threefold, " mutual assistance, the procreation of children, and the extinction of lust." Wherever these three objects had ceased to exist, divorce was, in his view and practice, allowable and should be granted by the judge

* Pufendorf, *Le Droit de la Nature et des Gens* (ed., 1759), II, vi, 1, 20 and foll.

in the exercise of his discretion. This view, he maintained, was not in conflict with the Scriptural texts, to which he was willing to allow the wide interpretation which Selden had given to them, for where all the ends of marriage had ceased to exist, the marriage was not so much dissolved as annulled by nature—an ingenious solution of the difficulty which is closely akin to the similar fiction employed by the Canon lawyers. It is clear, however, that this rule is as arbitrary as that of the various laws founded upon Scriptural interpretations, for it entirely ignored the wishes of the parties and had little regard for their welfare, although it was some advance upon the laws which the Reformers had made. For defects and radical differences of character between the parties Leyser would allow no remedy, for the parties, in his view, had only themselves to blame for their rashness in the choice of partners. Leyser was particularly harsh upon women in this matter, ignoring, of course, the fact that women in his day had little choice in the matter, while they could have little or no opportunity of discovering the character of the man to whom they were committing themselves for life. Long absence, however, he included under desertion, "for those who enjoin patience and chastity in such a case would think differently if they were in like circumstances." Excessive cruelty he also included under desertion, with which he compared it, though it does not appear that this opinion was ever acted upon by any of the courts which administered the Reformation laws. Incurable diseases, such as insanity, leprosy and impotence, and perpetual imprisonment and banishment, were valid grounds for divorce, and Leyser cites many instances from his own practice and that of the ecclesiastical courts of Germany where divorce was granted in such cases. Crimes involving other than capital punishment, however, Leyser disapproved of as grounds for divorce, for all the ends of marriage had not disappeared in such cases. He dissents from a decision in which the ecclesiastical court of one of the German towns had allowed a divorce to a woman whose husband had been condemned for some military crime by being branded and having his ears cut off—an opinion which exemplifies his own *dictum* that the theologians are sometimes more lenient than lawyers.*

In Denmark, Norway and Sweden, by the year 1750, similar grounds for divorce had been laid

* Leyser, *Meditationes ad Pandectas* (2nd ed., 1772), vol. V, *spec.* 290-318.

down by statute, as well as certain other serious crimes not involving the death penalty or perpetual banishment.* Scotland† and Holland, however, still adhered rigidly to the two Scriptural grounds alone. The Dutch, instead of adding other grounds for divorce in accordance with the Roman law, as Bynkershoek had suggested, extended malicious desertion as far, and made it as mild, as possible. Although Brouwer accepted the view of Selden, he was not prepared to allow divorce on the ground of any other crime than adultery and desertion, while insanity, being "a calamity, not a fault," was not considered to be warranted as a ground for divorce by the Scriptures. Voet, writing about 1700, says that marriage is not dissoluble on account of contagious disease or insanity, and cites the well-known moral *dictum* of the Roman law that nothing is so natural as that one spouse should share in the accidental misfortunes of the other. He is not prepared to follow the opinion of the Emperor Leo, because the Divine law nowhere pronounces insanity to be a just cause for divorce. The sane spouse is not allowed to marry, "in order that greater misfortunes may not be heaped upon one already afflicted and a

* Burge, 1st ed., I, ch. viii ; 2nd ed., III, 852-5.
† Collins *v.* Collins (1884), 9, A.C. 205.

fit subject for compassion than upon a criminal or guilty spouse." It is clear that the ruling principle of this opinion is a strict adherence to the letter of the Scriptures and the conception that divorce is in all cases a disgraceful thing. Compassion for the sane spouse is left out of account, and indeed the idea of compassion appears to be introduced solely to support the Scriptural interpretation. Van Leeuwen, who holds the same view, says that the marriage tie is retained in such a case " for the sake of conjugal faith and fellowship," though the insanity be hopeless and the insane spouse has to be confined in an asylum for the rest of his or her life. He also cites the Canon law in support of this. So the law remained in Holland till the beginning of the nineteenth century, when, owing to the influence of the French Revolution and the Roman law, the condemnation of either spouse to imprisonment or banishment for life or the commission of a heinous or unnatural offence were held by the Dutch courts to be good grounds for divorce. Van der Keessel considered that the commission of a heinous offence was an even stronger ground for divorce than adultery. Van der Linden, who held similar views, pointed out that judges were as unnecessarily scrupulous and reluctant to grant divorces as they were rash and negligent in confirming judicial separations.*

By this time the drastic criminal penalties which the Reformers had laid down for the guilty party had for the most part fallen into disuse. It was soon perceived that an adulterer who was forbidden re-marriage in his own country, either with his accomplice or with any other person, could, and often did, take up a domicile in some other country where he was unknown or which was more favourable to liberty. In the same way the penalties were either evaded or anticipated by flight, and the only effects of these rigid rules were to favour illicit connections and the birth of illegitimate children, to punish those who were not wealthy enough to seek re-marriage in another country, and to denude the country of some of its best citizens, who were unfortunate in their married life. Brouwer is therefore prepared to concede the right of re-marriage, which the Scriptures did not deny to an adulterer, but it must be " without pomp and festivity " and it should take place before a magistrate, " for no minister

* Brouwer, II, *cap. ult.*; J. Voet, *ad Pandectas*, 24, 2, 16; Van Leeuwen, *Censura Forensis*, 1, 1, 15, 5; Van der Keessel, *Select Theses*, 88-9; Van der Linden, *Institutes* I, 1, 9; Jooste v. Jooste, 24 S.C. 329, at pp. 331 and foll.

should be compelled to celebrate the marriages of those who have behaved so disgracefully in their former marriages "—the feelings of the second bride being unworthy of consideration. The forbidding of intermarriage between adulterers, however, still remained a pious statutory memorial of the Scriptural views of the Reformers. The party who was guilty of adultery or desertion, instead of being punished criminally, had merely to forego any proprietary advantages which he or she had derived from the marriage, as well as the custody of the children, which as a rule was granted to the innocent party. Generally the parties were by divorce placed in the same legal condition as they were in before the marriage, with the exception that one of them must of necessity be stigmatised by law and public opinion as the " guilty " party. Although crime was the sole ground for divorce, it rested with the innocent party whether he would sue for a divorce or forgive the guilty party. If the guilty party did not desire forgiveness, but divorce, he depended entirely upon the good-will of the innocent party. Anything like an agreement between the parties to obtain a divorce was punished as collusion and divorce refused to both. Similarly, although the crime of one was sufficient for a divorce, divorce was refused, where both had committed the same crime, for one party must be innocent and the other guilty, especially in the case of adultery. It is clear that the innocent party in the case of desertion was merely the one who happened to sue first. By a law of Prussia cited by Van Leeuwen, where the parties were present and had mutually deserted each other and left off living together, and one of them wished to give an opportunity for reconciliation, but the other refused to take it, if that other was " contumaciously " unwilling to obey, account had first to be taken whether he was rich, and then by imprisonment and other suitable penalties he should be compelled by the court to resume cohabitation. If even this stress did not effect its object, the innocent party should be given leave to marry again, while the other should be expelled from the province.*

Thus in most Protestant countries the wishes and welfare of the parties were practically excluded ; the Canon law of judicial separation and nullity of marriage was borrowed to eke out a law based upon an interpretation of the Scriptures which was entirely in conflict with that law, and marriage, though acknowledged to be a

* Brouwer, 2, 18 ; Voet, 24, 2, 5 ; Van Leeuwen, *Censura Forensis*, 1, 1, 15, 12.

civil contract, remained under the influence of dogmatists. In Catholic countries, where the Reformation had been extirpated by the Inquisition, the old Canon law remained in force. It is in France, a Catholic country, that the practical working-out of the more liberal ideas of divorce which have been noticed in the writings of eminent thinkers first took place, and it is to the French Revolution that the entire revolution which has taken place and is still taking place in the laws of divorce in all countries is principally due. The French kings had always successfully resisted the secular jurisdiction of the Popes, and the Canon law, though administered in France, had been for a long time under the exclusive jurisdiction of the royal courts. Calvin and Beza, the more democratic spirits of the Reformation, had been compelled by the Inquisition to put their ideas into practice in Switzerland, and later on Switzerland repaid France by sending Rousseau to apply the final spark to the Revolution. France had not been wanting in great lawyers who had severely criticised the Canon law, of whom one of the most distinguished was Cujas, who flourished at the time of the Reformation. Jean Coras, an eminent judge, who joined the Reformers and perished at Toulouse on account of his

145

religion, inquired how God could be said to join
fools and those who were carried away by their
lusts and were often of the most discordant
minds and characters. Pothier, the most celebrated French jurist of the eighteenth century,
insisted upon the purely contractual nature of
marriage so far as the law was concerned, and
said that according to French law marriage and
divorce were solely subject to secular jurisdiction.
The arguments of Bellarmine and the Jesuits
that marriage was a sacrament were in his
opinion frivolous, and only put forward in order
to give the Pope temporal power over it.
Originally Church and State were one, but with
the multiplication of religious sects and the
establishment of the " grand idea " of religious
toleration, marriage had been secularised. He
resents the interference of the priests in granting
dispensations, while he takes care to avoid the
anathema of the Council of Trent by saying that
it only applies to the sacrament of marriage and
does not affect the civil contract. While freely
criticising the opinions of the Fathers on
which the Canon law was based, he con-
tents himself, for the rest, by expounding the
Canon law as the actual law of France. By a
strange irony, although he clearly preferred
the Roman to the Canon law, his exposition of

the latter has had a considerable influence upon its perpetuation in France, especially in legal tradition.*

Montesquieu, one of the principal forerunners of the French Revolution, appears to have been the first French jurist to recommend a change in the divorce law. He continued the comparative and historical inquiry in the laws of the exponents of the Law of Nature, and in his *Spirit of the Laws* in 1748 he strongly advocated a return to the Roman law of divorce. He pointed out that the necessity for declaring a ground for divorce had been laid down for the first time by the Christian Emperors. " In the nature of the thing," he says, " the reasons for repudiation should be given [to the other party], while the reasons for divorce are unnecessary ; because whatever causes the law may admit as sufficient to break a marriage, a mutual antipathy must be stronger than them all." This brings us to the French Revolution, by which the principles of the Roman law were re-established.†

---

* Rittershusius, *de Differentiis*, I ; Pothier, *Mariage*, I, 3, and II, §§ 487-497 and *passim* ; Pothier, *ad Pandectas*, 24, 2.

† Montesquieu, *The Spirit of the Laws*, Book XVI, ch. 16.

VIII

THE FRENCH REVOLUTION AND ITS INFLUENCE

"Le consentement mutual et persévérant des epoux. . . prouvera suffisament que la vie commune leur est insupportable, et qu'il existe, par rapport à eux, une cause peremptoire de divorce."

—The mutual and persistent consent of the spouses. . . shall prove sufficiently that the common life is insupportable, and that there exists, with regard to them, a peremptory cause of divorce.—CODE CIVIL (1803), Art 233.

IF the absence of divorce is the sign of a healthy condition of morality, France before the Revolution was Utopia. History tells us, however, that though marriage was legally indissoluble under the *ancien régime*, it was frequently a merely nominal bond. It has been asserted that the French Revolutionists by freely allowing divorce sinned against the primary rules of morality and family life. "But why," asks Bishop, the eminent American authority, "were so many divorces sought? Did the corruption begin with the divorce law? . . . The truth is, that France had for so many centuries been under the Roman Catholic rule

151

of indissolubility, that social and matrimonial impunity had swollen to such a degree as at last to burst all bounds and overflow the country." The divorce law of the French Revolution was, as we have seen, " no meteor from the unknown," but, as Lord Acton says of the Revolution itself, " was the product of historic influences." The Revolutionists re-enacted the ancient laws of the Franks, the Roman law which had been in force till the Canon law displaced it, and the same law as had always been and still was in vogue in Switzerland, and which had been advocated, as we have seen, by the leading minds of Europe. The French Revolution proclaimed that men and women had rights as well as duties. Marriage was declared again to be a civil contract in which husband and wife were equal partners, and its registration, which had hitherto been in the hands of the priests, was placed in the hands of civil officials. A civil ceremony for the marriage contract, which already existed in England and had existed in Holland since the Reformation, was made obligatory. Marriage being based upon the consent and affection of the parties, it seemed only right that when that affection had ceased to exist, the parties should have the right to dissolve the contract either by mutual consent or at the will of either party,

152

like any other partnership. The Canonistic separation from bed and board was accordingly abolished and the parties were allowed to dissolve the contract with the sanction of the court, which merely registered their will and did not inquire into the secret causes of the divorce, either by mutual consent or on the allegation of one party alone that the parties were incompatible. The aversion of the French to any public inquiry into the causes of divorce and the secrets of family life was proverbial, and even where one party charged the other with some crime the investigation of the facts was entrusted to a family council. "It is," says Mr. Fisher, in the *Cambridge Modern History*, "a curious fact in human nature that the experiment of entrusting these delicate inquiries to the family council broke down, not so much by reason of the incompetence of its members as because of their sheer indifference to an issue in which their sentiments should have been closely involved." The fact is, however, not so curious as it appears, for besides the inherent improbability of a tribunal composed of relatives being able to come to an agreement, it must be remembered that, as divorce could be obtained without the necessity of any inquiry into the conduct of either party, the family council must have been rarely resorted to. The same historian says " that a contract should be abolished at the will of the parties was in itself an anomaly "—a statement which shows that the legal and personal opinions of historians are not always as safe a guide as the facts which they narrate.*

After the French Revolution had " devoured her children," the priests and lawyers, who had controlled marriage and divorce for centuries, began to recover some of their lost power. When Napoleon entrusted the preparation of his famous Civil Code to the lawyers it was found that most of them retained the old Canonistic preference for judicial separation and the public inquiry into the causes of divorce, for they naturally desired to recover the control of litigation, which had been for so long a time a source of profit and power. The devotion of lawyers to tradition is a commonplace of history, and the French lawyers turned as naturally to the " old and pertinacious tradition of French jurisprudence " as the lawyers of the Reformation period turned to the Canon law. Most of them, as Mr. Fisher tells us, rejected the assertion of

* *Cambridge Modern History*, X, vi, p. 157, and see the whole chapter for a valuable account of the legislation ; Bishop, § 44 & foll.; *Cambridge Modern History*, VIII, ch. xxiv, pp. 736 and foll.

incompatibility of temper as a ground for divorce, and more than one tribunal stipulated that incompatibility must be proved in open court. Incompatibility of temper was therefore ruled out of the Code, and many provisions were inserted in it to conciliate both the lawyers and the Catholic priests, with whom Napoleon wished to be on friendly terms. It was mainly owing to the influence of Napoleon that the fundamental principle of the divorce laws of the Revolution, divorce by mutual consent, was retained in the Code. Napoleon was strongly of opinion that " divorce for specific causes would not be sufficient. The offences contemplated were not only difficult to prove, but in the attempt to prove them, the wronged and the wrong-doer were alike dragged into publicity." He thought that the dissolution of marriage should be not only more private, but more honourable, and more in accordance with public opinion. " Divorce by mutual consent for incompatibility of temper was in his view essential to marital happiness. Girls married young . . . In most cases a young girl fresh from school or convent could not know whether her husband would prove congenial ; in most cases a marriage was an affair of convenience. It was well that, when mistakes were made, they should be capable

of being corrected without noise or scandal."
Judicial separation was "a bad expedient, for
it involved publicity and favoured immoral
conduct," and was at best only a middle course
for the upper classes. Napoleon was a strong
upholder of the integrity and morality of the
family, which he looked upon, as all rulers have
looked upon it, as a political or military institution which can more easily be ruled where the
husband is the absolute head, and it can scarcely
be contended that he ever feared that either
family or morality would suffer by a liberal law
of divorce. By allowing divorce by mutual consent and for cruelty, and by advocating divorce
on the ground of incompatibility even where
the wife alone desired it, Napoleon did more for
married women than had ever been done since
Roman times, although in other respects he
placed wives in subjection to the head of the
family and placed women in subjection in many
other ways for political and military reasons.
Napoleon appears to have made a genuine
attempt to codify the popular will on the subject
of divorce, and the arbitrary rules which were
introduced by the lawyers are not to be attri-
buted to him. It cannot be said that in all
this Napoleon had his own future divorce in
view, because when he divorced Josephine ten

years later he " dispensed with the formalities of the Civil Code," * but obtained a decree from a subservient Senate and an equally subservient Archbishop, as Henry VIII of England, and thirteen French kings from the time of Charlemagne, had done before him. Like Henry VIII of England, he divorced his wife because he wanted a legitimate male-heir, and, like that monarch, he had every reason to believe that the fault was not upon his side. While, however, his attempts to found a dynasty failed, together with his attempt to found a European Empire, his Code remains, as Mr. Fisher says, " the most durable and certainly not the least surprising manifestation of Napoleon's energy." †

In the Code, as it was finally promulgated in 1803, the lawyers and Catholics succeeded in retaining a great deal of the Canon law and in hedging round divorce with as many arbitrary difficulties and delays as possible. As one eminent authority says, " the original procedure prescribed by the Code Civil for cases of divorce was purposely made complicated in order to render the dissolution of marriage a matter of difficulty. . . . In practice this procedure in-

* *Cambridge Modern History*, IX, pp. 139, 140.
† *Cambridge Modern History*, *ubi supra*; Lecky, *Democracy and Liberty*, II, pp. 152 and foll.

volved a great expense and waste of judicial time "—to say nothing of the waste of time and the inconvenience to the parties themselves. The parties who wished to be divorced by mutual consent, though they had been capable of contracting the marriage, were, when they both wished to dissolve it, treated as children, requiring the consent of their parents or other surviving ancestors. On their first appearance in court, accompanied by their respective lawyers, whose presence was essential, they had to make a declaration that they and their said ancestors consented to the divorce, and that they had come to an arrangement as to the care and custody of the children and the division of their property. The judge then delivered a lecture to them upon the serious effects of the course which they were adopting, one of which was that after divorce they would never be able to marry each other again, accompanied by " such exhortations as to him seemed advisable." This paternal procedure had to be repeated on three other occasions during the course of a year, at the end of which time, if their funds and patience were not exhausted, a decree of divorce was granted. After the divorce neither party was allowed to marry again until three years had elapsed. This divorce was not allowed in any case until after two years' trial of married life, or later than twenty, or after the wife had turned forty-five years of age, even if she desired it.*

Besides divorce by mutual consent, divorce was allowed upon certain grounds, which, owing to the same Catholic influences, were narrowed down to adultery, cruelty and condemnation for certain serious crimes. Here also the procedure was made difficult, expensive and full of delays, three appearances in court during the course of a year being necessary. Most of the old Canonistic distinctions between the rights of husband and wife and the restrictions as to the re-marriage of one of the parties were restored. The wife was said to owe obedience to her husband while he owed her his protection. This protection, however, was in most cases a legal fiction, for her so-called protector could commit adultery as often as he liked, so long as he did not do it in the home. If the wife endeavoured to escape from a degraded husband by committing adultery herself, she was liable to imprisonment for two years after being divorced, and was never allowed to marry her "accomplice." She was also, whether guilty or not, forbidden to marry in

* Burge (2nd ed.), III, p. 832 ; Code Civil (ed., 1815), Arts. 233, 275-80, 295, 297.

M

any case until six months after divorce. The parties to a divorce, for any cause, were also forbidden to intermarry again. The innocent spouse as a rule obtained the custody of the children, though the court had a discretion in the matter. Judicial separation, or, as it was called, "Catholic divorce," was retained, but only as an alternate remedy and only upon the same grounds and according to the same procedure as divorce. The important principle of the conversion of judicial separation into divorce, after the lapse of three years, and on the application of one of the parties, was introduced into the law, though even here the wife who had been guilty of adultery was forbidden to obtain the conversion if the husband still desired to punish her with enforced celibacy.*

The Code Civil, with all its arbitrary restrictions and distinctions, was still a distinct advance upon the Canon law and the laws made by the Reformers. Divorce by mutual consent and the convertibility of judicial separation into divorce, which have had a lasting influence upon the laws of divorce in many countries, had been asserted, and the dogma of the indissolubility of marriage had received its death-blow. The Code Civil may be called the political testament

* Code Civil, Arts. 213, 229 and foll., 234, 296, 298-302, 306-310.

of Napoleon. In France itself, after the fall of Napoleon, and the restoration of the Catholic Bourbons in 1816, divorce was abolished altogether, and the Canon law prevailed again in France till 1884, when the divorce of the Code Civil was re-enacted with the exception of divorce by mutual consent. Since that time the procedure has been simplified and made exactly the same as in any other civil action; husband and wife have been placed on exactly the same footing, and all the Canonistic restrictions against remarriage have been abolished. Cruelty has been liberally interpreted by the courts to mean desertion, the refusal of marital rights, the existence of a contagious disease in either party, refusal of support on the part of the husband or of obedience on the part of the wife, unreasoning jealousy and habitual drunkenness. The Catholic Church appears to have now lost all political influence in France, and as that influence has always retarded divorce reform, it cannot be said that the French have said their last word upon the subject of divorce.*

In other countries the influence of the French Revolution and of the Code Napoléon has been

* Burge (2nd ed.), III, pp. 830-7 ; *Reports on Marriage and Divorce Laws in Foreign Countries* (1894) , part 2, pp. 67-71 ; *Law Quarterly Review*, vol. I, p. 355 (1885), article by T. Barclay ; Roger & Sorel, *Codes et Lois Usuelles* (1897).

more continuous. The Code Napoléon remained in force in the colony of Mauritius till 1872, when divorce by mutual consent was abolished by the British Government. The Code also became law, shortly after its promulgation, in Holland, Belgium, the whole of Germany, with the exception of Prussia, and Italy, including even the papal states. Italy, however, which has not known liberty till very recent times, soon returned to the Canon law. In 1809 the Code was proclaimed in Holland, except that divorce by mutual consent was not adopted, while desertion was retained in the Dutch law. The present Dutch Code, which dates from 1838, is in the same terms, with the important exception that judicial separations, which may be by mutual consent, are convertible after five years' duration, into divorces.*

Upon the confederation of the German states divorce by mutual consent was retained in those States where it had been established by Napoleon. In Prussia, what practically amounts to divorce by mutual consent had its origin independently of the French Revolution in the legislation of Frederick the Great and his great

* *Wetboek Napoleon*, arts. 199-223 ; Fruin, *Burgerlijke Wetboek*, arts. 254-290. In undefended cases no evidence is taken and judgment given by default where the defendant is absent. See *Reports on the Laws of Marriage and Divorce* (1894), part II, pp. 96-100.

Chancellor, Samuel von Cocceji. Cocceji had, as early as 1740, stated in an authoritative book that divorce by mutual consent as in the Roman law was in accordance with the Law of Nature, and had been nowhere forbidden by the Scriptures, which merely restricted the right of divorce, if they restricted it at all, where it was done against the will of the other party. He accordingly allowed divorce either by consent or on such grounds as capital enmities, other grave crimes, and certain serious diseases. These grounds had, he said, been allowed by the Christian Emperors of Rome, without any objection on the part of the Fathers of the Church, who would have been only too ready to express their dissent if such grounds had been contrary to the Scriptures. He accepted the views of Selden and Grotius, and said that though in judicial practice there were only two grounds for divorce as of right (adultery and desertion), the sovereign had full power of dispensation to allow divorce for any just cause, such as disease, as frequently happened in Germany, with the approval of the Reformed theologians. The Prussian Code, however, which Frederick had ordered to be made, and in which Cocceji took a prominent part, did not see the light until after his death, in 1791. In this Code, divorce

was allowed by mutual consent on the ground
of incompatibility of temper, although the
judge appears to have had the power of inquiring into the causes of the incompatibility,
and to have had the discretion to grant a
divorce in any case where, in his opinion,
there was some rooted dislike between the
parties so as to make reconciliation hopeless.
Divorce by mutual consent remained in force
throughout Germany until 1900, when it was
abolished by the new Code, and the grounds
for divorce are now adultery, desertion for one
year, insanity, designs by the one upon the life
of the other, or if either spouse " by grave violation of the duties of marriage, or by dishonourable
or immoral conduct, has caused so grave a dis-
order of the matrimonial relation that the
spouse cannot be presumed to continue the
marriage. Gross maltreatment is also regarded
as such grave violation." These provisions
represent a political compromise to meet the
views of Protestants and Catholics alike. The
principle of the conversion of judicial separation
into divorce, at the request of either party after
the lapse of a certain time, has also been adopted
in Germany, and divorce is allowed even where
both parties are guilty of adultery. These laws
cannot be said to represent the views of the

German people, which had little or no voice in their making.*

Belgium has always retained the Code Napoléon, and divorce by mutual consent is still in force in that Catholic and democratic country. Roumania has also adopted the Code Napoléon with the exception of judicial separation, which it does not recognise. The Austrian Code of 1811, which is still in force, allows divorce by mutual consent in the case of all non-Catholics, wherever it is proved to the court that the parties are incompatible. Divorce is also allowed where adultery, a crime involving five years' imprisonment, desertion, invincible aversion, cruelty or an attempt by one upon the life of the other is proved. For Catholics, however, judicial separation is the only remedy, even where one or both of the parties have renounced that religion. In Spain and the republics of South America, the Canon law remains. During the revolutionary period, when King Ferdinand entered Valencia, the cathedral clergy requested

* Burge (1st ed.) I, pp. 640 and foll. (2nd ed.), III, pp. 890-1, 839, 844 ; Lodge, *History of Modern Europe* (popular ed.), p. 368 ; *Cambridge Modern History*, VI, p. 278, and *passim* ; *Journal of the Society of Comp. Legislation*, IX (N.S.), p. 88 ; and XIII (N.S.), p. 153, where Mr. Hirschfeld tells the story of the introduction of judicial separation and the part which the representatives of Bavaria played, at one time threatening to wreck the whole code (Löewy's *German Code*, arts. 1564 to 1587, esp. 1565-9 (grounds for divorce).

him to take the most vigorous measures for the restoration of the Inquisition and of the ecclesiastical system which had existed in Spain before the constitution of 1812. "These," replied that most Catholic monarch, "are my own wishes, and I will not rest until they are fulfilled." The Canon law, therefore, remains in force, though, as in Brazil and Mexico, judicial separation is granted where there is mutual consent, and marriage is legally a civil contract. In Portugal the Canon law remained in force until 1910, when the new Republic passed a law allowing divorce either by mutual consent or upon the grounds of adultery, desertion, living apart for ten years, insanity, absence for four years without news, inveterate gambling and certain diseases.*

In Denmark the laws of the Reformation, as extended by judicial interpretation, have generally been maintained, except that since 1839, "three years' actual living apart in accordance with a decree of separation" entitles either

* Burge (2nd ed.), III, pp. 837-9, 841-2 and *passim* ; Prof. E. Tilsch in the *Journal of the Society of Comp. Legislation* (1911), vol. XXV (N.S.), pp. 44 and foll.; Lodge, *A History of Modern Europe* (popular ed.), p. 373 ; *Reports on the Marriage and Divorce Laws* (1894), part II, pp. 21, 33, 46, 140. In the Argentine, a bill introducing divorce was lost in 1903 by two votes (Report of 1903, p. 4 ;) Decree of the Portuguese Republic, 3rd Nov., 1910, proclaimed also in Portuguese East Africa : Mutual guilt does not exclude divorce in Portugal, while judicial separation is convertible after one year into divorce.

party to a divorce, which practically means divorce by mutual consent. In Norway and Sweden since 1810 the King or the Minister of Justice has had power to grant divorce on the ground of incompatibility of temper or " where such differences are proved to exist between the parties as to cause mutual detestation and hatred," after the parties have lived apart for a year. In the case of Norway this discretion of the Minister of Justice has been made into a law which allows divorce as of right where both parties desire it and continue to live apart for one year, after a preliminary separation by a magistrate, which is granted where both parties desire it. Where one party only desires the divorce it may be granted without the necessity of stating any ground, and is always granted on such grounds as make it probable that all mutual goodwill is ruined.* Husband and wife are placed upon perfect equality, the wife upon divorce being entitled in all cases to one-half of the property, and where the divorce is not caused by her fault, the husband is required to support her after divorce. The custody of the children is at the discretion of the court, the wife being as a

* *E.g.*, drunkenness, insanity, gross neglect of conjugal duties or incompatibility. Mutual guilt does not exclude the right. (M. Castberg, former Minister of Justice of Norway, in *Nineteenth Century and After*, No. 420 (Feb., 112), pp. 364 and foll.).

rule entitled to the care and custody of young
children.   As Frü Anker says, the main principle
of this law, which was passed by the co-operation
of all parties, is that "only love is sacred, and
it is the deep companionship which love pro-
duces between husband and wife that gives
marriage any value." Mutual love and respect
between husband and wife is, according to this
law, the only moral basis of marriage, and where
this feeling fails or is seriously shaken, the law
ought to give the possibility of divorce." The
law recognises that divorce is "a relief from
misfortune, not a crime," and that the continuance of a marriage, where there is no mutual love
and respect, is injurious to morality, to the
individuals concerned, to society and to marriage
itself.   In Switzerland, divorce by mutual consent has always been in force from the earliest
times, "if in the opinion of the tribunal the
continuation of the common life is incompatible
with the nature of marriage." *

*Burge, 2nd ed. III, pp. 825-6 ; Frü Ella Anker, in a Lecture
delivered at Manchester ; *Weekly Scotsman*, Nov. 4th, 1911 ; Burge 2nd
ed., vol. III, 31 and 848 ; *Reports on the Laws of Marriage and Divorce*
(1894), part II, pp. 146 and foll.

IX

ENGLAND

"Why should Scotland be just and generous to women in this respect, and England cold, unfeeling, barbarous?"

LORD LYNDHURST.

THE history of divorce in England before the Reformation is similar to that of the rest of Western Europe, the Canon law introduced by William I displacing the ancient customs. Before the Norman Conquest divorce had been freely allowed to either party both by the English Kings and by the English Church. By the Penitentials of Theodore, who was Archbishop of Canterbury from 668 to 698 A.D., marriages were declared to be dissoluble either by mutual consent or on the grounds of desertion, adultery, impotence, relationship, long absence and captivity.*

The Reformation in England was brought about by the divorce of Henry VIII from Catherine of Aragon. The story of the divorces of Henry VIII are too well known to need more than a brief mention. A marriage had been arranged and had taken place between Henry, when a mere

---

* *Ancient Laws and Institutes of England,* containing *Laws of Ethelbert,*§§ 79, 80, and *Liber Pœnitentialis Theodori,* p. 11 and foll., XVI 23, 28, XIX 18, 20, 23, 24, 31 : Divorce was enjoined where there was adultery or desertion ; Holdsworth, *History of Eng. Law,* vol. 2, p. 78. See pp. 82-86, *supra.*

youth, and Catherine, mainly because of political considerations. As she was the widow of Henry's brother, a dispensation allowing the marriage had been obtained from the Pope. After some years of married life, Henry, who was desirous of obtaining a male-heir who would strengthen the succession to the throne, despaired of obtaining one from Catherine, and ceased to live with her. After about two years of such separation his conscience, it is said, began to trouble him, for he feared that all this while he had been "living in sin," in spite of the Pope's dispensation. He therefore sought legal opinions throughout Europe as to the validity of his marriage. No fewer than two hundred opinions of the doctors confirmed him in his view that the marriage had never really taken place, that no one on earth could alter God's law, which forbade marriages where there was so close a relationship, and that he was entitled to either divorce her or take an additional wife. For about five years he endeavoured to obtain a divorce from the Pope, who was willing to grant a divorce if Catherine consented to it and facilitated matters by taking a formal vow of chastity. She, however, refused to give up the royal dignity, maintaining that her marriage was valid and indissoluble. It was then suggested that in order to avoid the divorce, their daughter, afterwards Queen Mary, should marry the young Duke of Richmond, an illegitimate son of Henry, so as to make the succession to the throne more secure, and the Pope was prepared to grant a dispensation for that marriage. Henry by this time had become engaged to Anne Boleyn, and he was quite prepared to discard her in that event. Nothing, however, came of these negotiations, and the Pope sent a legate to England ostensibly to try the question of Henry's marriage. No decision was arrived at, for the Pope feared to offend the Emperor, upon whom he was politically dependent, and who was closely related to Catherine. At length Henry became impatient of the prolongation of his cause by the Holy See, and as by this time Anne Boleyn gave promise of a child, who he hoped would be a son, he took the matter into his own hands. He commissioned the Archbishop of Canterbury and other bishops to try the case, and they granted him a divorce, which was confirmed by both houses of Convocation and by Parliament, and the children of the former marriage were declared to be illegitimate. The Pope, therefore, excommunicated him, and England seceded from the Church of Rome. As Anne did not bear him a son, but a daughter, afterwards Queen Elizabeth, Henry soon divorced her on the ground of an alleged impediment to their marriage in the form of a pre-contract between her and the Earl of Northumberland, and she was afterwards beheaded because of her supposed adultery. A few months after the death of his third wife he married Anne of Cleves, and being dissatisfied with her after six months divorced her. This divorce was in reality by mutual consent, but the ostensible ground was that the King had never " inwardly consented " to the marriage.*

When England had separated from the Church of Rome the Canon law was allowed to remain in force in the ecclesiastical courts, although its authority was restricted and its study at the Universities was forbidden. Henry, however, as we have seen, found it convenient to him in his divorces, and many of his subjects also did so. At this time (1540) divorce was very frequent and " mightily prevailed," as Strype tells us. " For it was ordinary to annul marriages and divide man and wife from each other

---

* Froude, *Life and Letters of Erasmus* (1906 ed.), pp. 376 & foll., 416 & foll. ; Froude, *The Divorce of Catherine of Aragon*, where the whole story is detailed ; J. Strype, *Memorials of Cranmer*, pp. 18-22, 48-49, 319-320 ; *Cambridge Modern History*, II, ch. xi, *esp.* pp. 440-453 ; Blackstone, 15th ed., p. 435.

who, it may be, had lived together and had children in wedlock; when upon any disgust of man and wife they would withdraw themselves from one another, and so in effect make their children bastards, upon pretence of some pre-contract or affinity, which by the Pope's law required divorce." The King, who was by this time glutted with divorces, " took particular care " of an Act which had been drawn up and was passed declaring all validly constituted marriages to be indissoluble. This Act did not, however, meet the mischief, as probably the King intended it should not, for the loophole was still left of annulling marriages by the Canon law.*

As the Canon law " extolled the Pope unmeasurably," Henry in 1549 appointed a Commission to " rough-hew " it, and compile a new body of ecclesiastical laws more in conformity with a Church and a kingdom which had emerged from the " vale of darkness." This Commission consisted of Archbishop Cranmer, Latimer and other eminent divines and lawyers who drew up the famous Reform of the Ecclesiastical Laws (*Reformatio Legum*). By its provisions divorce was to be granted by the ecclesiastical courts on the grounds of adultery, desertion, long

* J. Strype, *ubi supra*, p. 80 ; Blackstone, *loc. cit.*

N

absence, cruelty, an attempt upon the life of one of the spouses by the other, or deadly hatred between the spouses, while separation from bed and board was to be abolished. Incurable disease was not allowed as a ground for divorce. Husband and wife were placed upon the same footing, the innocent party was allowed to marry, while the guilty party was subjected to the usual drastic penalties such as banishment, which all the Reformers usually inflicted in such cases. This proposed law of divorce was based on the Canon law and upon the views which were commonly held by the Reformers and had been put in practice in other countries. With the exception of allowing divorce instead of judicial separation, and allowing divorce where the parties hated one another so as to prevent them from either murdering or attempting to murder one another, as some of the Fathers and Christian Emperors had also provided, there was nothing new in this scheme of reform. This reformation would in all probability have become law if Henry had not died. His successor Edward VI indeed ratified it, but Parliament refused to make it law, not from any want of confidence in its utility, but solely because the Commons objected to spiritual jurisdiction of any kind, " whether it was exercised by Catholic or

Protestant prelates." As Strype says, " all this great and long labour of the Archbishop came to no effect by reason of the King's untimely death, and, it may be, the secret opposition of the Papists." Thus England, by an accident, failed not only to adopt a law of divorce which in some respects anticipates modern legislation but to adopt any law of divorce at all, and by a strange irony the Catholic Canon law was allowed to quietly resume its old authority in a Protestant country.*

Both before and after this report was drawn up divorce was frequent. Strype tells us that " noblemen would very frequently put away their wives and marry others if they like another woman better or were like to obtain wealth by her. And they would sometimes pretend their former wives to be false to their beds and so be divorced and marry again such as they fancied." Thus the Earl of Pembroke divorced his wife and married a daughter of Sir Philip Sidney. So frequent indeed did divorce become that it was at one time proposed to bring in an Act to punish adultery by death. Perhaps the most celebrated case is that of the Earl of

* J. Strype, pp. 132-4 ; Bishop, §§ 30 & 661-2, and Burge (1910), iii, p. 861, and authorities there cited. A useful summary of the provisions of the *Reformatio Legum* is given in the *Quarterly Review*, Oct., 1911, *esp.* pp. 543-4 ; *Cambridge Modern History*, II. ch. xv.

Northampton, who, while the commission was pursuing its inquiries, obtained a divorce from his wife in one of the episcopal courts on the ground of her adultery. Ten bishops, of whom Cranmer was one, were appointed at the beginning of Edward's reign to inquire whether, according to God's law, the Earl should be allowed to marry again. Archbishop Cranmer, who, besides being principally responsible for the proposed reform of the divorce laws, was the principal compiler of the English Book of Common Prayer, went very carefully into the history of divorce and wrote a book, in which he maintained that re-marriage in such cases was not contrary to the Scriptures or to the practice of the Early Church, and that the denial of re-marriage was a late encroachment by the Popes. The majority of the bishops agreed with this view, and the second marriage of the impatient Earl, which had taken place in the interval, was declared to be in accordance with the divine law. The Earl afterwards obtained a private Act of Parliament confirming the divorce, which was the first instance of that kind of procedure with the exception of Henry VIII's own divorces. This Act was afterwards annulled when the Earl had fallen into royal disfavour. When Mary ascended the throne and the

Inquisition and the Canon law were put into active operation, " many thousands " of married clergymen were divorced by the ecclesiastical courts from their wives, or rather their " women, as the Papists now chose to style them," by royal command, and were punished and deprived of their livings. All married clergymen were commanded "to bring their wives within a fortnight that they might be divorced from them." Many of them were obliged to publicly confess, in accordance with a prescribed formula, that their marriages had been contrary to the canons and customs of the Universal Church, that they had been living with them " to the evil example of all good Christian people," and that they were now ashamed of their conduct and promised never to return to their " women " either as wives or concubines.* Public indignation was aroused at these proceedings, but public opinion had no means of voicing itself, and was in the same position as " John Nobody that durst not speak," as the old ballad said. Great care was taken by the advisers of Mary to get " Parliament men that might do what was to be laid before them." In the reigns of Edward VI and Elizabeth, however, divorces continued to

* The Statute of Six Articles of Henry VIII, which forbade the marriage of priests, had also been followed by numerous divorces of married priests. (Lea, *Sacerdotal Celibacy*, p. 486).

179

be granted by the ecclesiastical courts in accordance with the *Reformatio Legum* and the ancient custom of the realm, at any rate on the ground of adultery, and no one questioned the right of the parties to re-marry until near the end of Elizabeth's reign in 1601, when the Star Chamber, presided over by the then Archbishop, by what appears to have been a doubtful exercise of jurisdiction, declared that marriage was by English law indissoluble, as Henry VIII had declared it, and that no court had the power to dissolve a validly subsisting marriage. From that time the ecclesiastical courts only granted judicial separations, or declared marriages null and void and the children consequently illegitimate on such grounds as impotence or under one of the many fictions of the Canon law. To remedy the *impasse* caused by the decision of the Star Chamber, the practice of divorce by private Act of Parliament, following the precedents of the Earl of Northampton and Henry VIII and "agreeably to what the *Reformatio Legum* did propose," as Burn says, was reintroduced in the reign of Charles II, the first case being that of Lord Roos, who was afterwards the Earl of Rutland, in 1669. That noble lord had obtained a judicial separation from his wife in an episcopal court on the ground of her alleged

180

adultery. The Act of Parliament confirmed the divorce and granted leave to the Earl to re-marry, and her children were declared illegitimate, although it appeared that he had left her destitute for years before the alleged adultery. This practice was continued and remained the only mode by which divorce was obtainable in England until 1857.*

Before a private Act could be obtained, it was necessary first to obtain a judicial separation in an ecclesiastical court, in which the plaintiff had to enter into a purely nominal bond that he or she would not marry again during the lifetime of the divorced spouse. The husband, if he were plaintiff, had also to bring an action for damages against the person with whom his wife had committed adultery, for trespass to the husband in his marital property, an action in which the wife had no right to be a party. A private Act of Parliament always originated in the House of Lords, where the Bishops had practical control over all divorce bills, and before the Act was passed a provision was invariably inserted in it, and invariably struck out, that the innocent party would not marry

* Burnet's *Hist. of the Reformation* (ed. 1865), II, p. 117, and III, p. 362 & foll.; *History of his Own Time* (ed. Airy), I, pp. 471-2, and notes; Burn, *Eccles. Law* (1824) II, pp. 496 *ff*; Strype, pp. 205, 326-344, and appendices.

again, although it was clear that if the plaintiff
had intended to remain celibate he would not
have gone to all the trouble of obtaining a divorce.   The Bishops do not appear to have ever
objected to this procedure, except in the
notorious case of the Duke of Norfolk, in 1694,
when some of them opposed the passing of the
bill.   In that case, however, political feeling
ran high, for the wife was " a Papist and a busy
Jacobite." *   By this cumbrous and expensive
procedure and multiplication of actions, women
and all but the wealthiest persons were practically debarred from obtaining a remedy, only
four cases of divorce in favour of women having
ever been granted by Act of Parliament, in all
of which either bigamy or incest was an additional element to the husband's adultery.†

The principal cause of the Divorce Act of 1857
was the widespread discontent at the ecclesiastical courts, which had an extensive jurisdiction
not only over matrimonial causes, but over
many other matters also, such as defamation, with
wide powers of fine and imprisonment, which
they freely exercised.   The abuses caused by
these courts had been pointed out by Sir Samuel
Romilly at the beginning of the nineteenth

---

* Burnet, *History of his Own Time* (1818 ed.), III, p. 139.
† Hansard, *Parliamentary Debates*, vol. 147, p. 1541.

century, but they refused to reform themselves, and even Lord Chancellors were chary of interfering with such powerful interests. It was not until 1853 that a Commission was appointed to inquire into the working of these courts. This commission reported, *inter alia*, that, although a validly contracted marriage was by English law indissoluble by any court, yet the mutual dissolution of such a contract, where adultery was committed, was so consonant to reason and religion, that where the general law had failed to give a remedy, Parliament had stepped in to provide one specially by passing a private law in favour of those who could make out a case which would warrant its interference, and by this means the right to obtain divorce was " definitely established." The Commission does not appear to have inquired into the advisability -of adding to the grounds for divorce, and the bill which was framed upon their findings did not purport to make any new law upon the subject, but was merely intended, as the Attorney-General said, " to erect a new tribunal and to embody the principles of the law which already existed." This law, as we have seen, was practically the Canon law. The provisions of the Divorce Act of 1857, amended in some slight particulars by a later Act, are well known. The jurisdiction of the ecclesiastical courts was taken away and divorce placed under the jurisdiction of the (now) Supreme Court. The husband is entitled to divorce his wife on the ground of her adultery and to sue for damages against the co-respondent. The wife, however, can only obtain a divorce where she proves, in addition to her husband's adultery, his desertion, cruelty, bigamy or incest, while she has no corresponding action for damages. The court has a discretion to refuse divorce wherever the plaintiff is guilty of a serious matrimonial offence, or where there is any assistance by one of the parties to the other's obtaining a divorce, an official known as the King's Proctor having the duty of inquiring into such matters and opposing a final decree of divorce in such cases. Besides this, judicial separation and nullity of marriage may be obtained by either spouse upon the grounds laid down by the Canon law.* This Act, as the Attorney-General stated, was not intended to be the end-all of legislation upon the subject, for by the bill a tribunal would be created which might hereafter have to administer laws made under happier auspices, although he admitted

* Browne, *Divorce and Matrimonial Causes*, 4th ed. ; 20 & 21 Vict., c. 85. The other grounds for divorce given in § 27 of the Act cannot be said to be Scriptural.

that the position of women under it " might be called opprobrious and wicked." The Government refused to discuss the merits of other grounds for divorce or the position of women, having in the abolition of the traditional privileges of the bishops a sufficiently difficult political undertaking, especially as the bishops strongly opposed the bill altogether, while the men who were in Parliament were not prepared in any way to forego their legal superiority over women.

The story of the debate as told in Hansard, although it is instructive, is- not pleasant reading. The strenuous opposition of the bishops not only to the bill but to any amendment of it which did not further restrict the rights of women, can only be explained by the fact that their privileges were about to come to an end, and because they were opposed to the re-marriage of divorced persons in Church. The latter question aroused considerable opposition in both Houses and was the principal cause of a great deal of theological argument, and it was only removed by a compromise suggested by Mr. Gladstone, allowing individual clergymen, by a sort of conscientious objector's clause, the right of refusing to celebrate such marriages, though not taking away the right of such persons to be

married in the Church. The desire of the
bishops to protect the privileges and consciences
of the clergy entirely outweighed the necessity
of amending a long-standing grievance, especially
as regards women and poor people whose position
was not improved by the bill. The bishops,
especially the famous Samuel Wilberforce,
Bishop of Oxford, not only aimed at retaining
all the old ecclesiastical inequalities between
the rights of husband and wife, but even at introducing further elements of injustice against
the wife. They advocated a provision by which,
when the wife was sued for divorce, it should
be refused where the husband was himself guilty
of adultery. Adultery was to be made a criminal
offence, and the guilty wife forbidden intermarriage with the co-respondent. It was
pointed out by more than one temporal peer
that all these restrictions operated to the detri-
ment of the wife, who would be left by them in
a worse position than the lowest criminal, without any possible hope of amending her social
position, while the man who had seduced her
would be glad to be rid of the moral obligation
of marrying the woman whom he had by his
seduction excluded from society while he remained
an honourable member of it. The Bishop of
Oxford admitted that as a rule the woman gave

her husband ground for divorce, " not because of the direct temptations of appetite, but in ninety-nine cases out of a hundred she fell because her marriage had been unhappy in its consequences." Not one bishop maintained that marriage was by the law of God indissoluble ; all admitted that it was dissoluble in certain cases. The Bishop of Exeter thought it advisable to remind the House that Constantine had refused divorce to the wife unless there were in addition to adultery "certain other ingredients in the case," but did not add that not only were other grounds for divorce open to her by that law, but that divorce by mutual consent was not considered by the first Christian Emperor to be contrary to the Christian religion. The same bishop objected to judicial separation as it was a Catholic institution, which should not be permanently inflicted upon Protestants. The Bishop of St. Davids objected to the bill altogether because Christ had not made any laws at all, but had left the matter to the discretion of legislatures, and he contended that the legislatures should act according to the spirit of the Scriptures and not according to particular words contained in them, but he made no attempt, as Mr. Gladstone afterwards did, for the same reason, to amend the law in any way.

A HISTORY OF DIVORCE

" *Video meliora proboque ; deteriora sequor.*"

The lay lords and law lords generally, with a few exceptions, said all that they knew, although they did not do much, to remedy what they acknowledged to be the injustice of the law. The Lord Chancellor proposed that deeds of separation should be legalised. Lord Lyndhurst was, however, practically the only man in the House of Lords who went to any trouble to amend the law in accordance with legislation in other countries. Mrs. Norton, the famous authoress, had been falsely accused by her husband of adultery with Lord Melbourne, and after the failure of the charge was compelled to remain married to him, though she separated from him after enduring for a long time his cruelty and misconduct, while he, who was a magistrate, made use of his knowledge of the law to deprive her of her children and even of her literary earnings. It was mainly because he was fired by the intense sufferings of this fearless and brilliant womën that Lord Lyndhurst, who had been many times Lord Chancellor, so ably championed the cause of women in the matter that Mr. Gladstone afterwards said of his argument that it would puzzle the wit of man to answer it. His effective disposal of the Scriptural arguments has been already noticed, especially the manner in which he dealt with the supposed authority of St. Augustine for the indissolubility of marriage.* He cited Grotius, Selden, Erasmus and Cranmer in support of the extension of the grounds of divorce. He refuted the argument that the extension of the grounds for divorce would have a bad effect upon the morality of the poorer classes, and said that on the contrary the denial of divorce led to acts of brutal violence against women. He strongly advocated that desertion should be made a ground for divorce and that husband and wife should have equal rights, as in Scotland. It was not only their duty to protect the poor, but to protect women, who had no means of protecting themselves. By marriage a woman gave up everything, and when abandoned by the object of her affection she saw nothing before her but a dreary existence without anything upon which she could repose her affections. " Hope never comes that comes to all." †

Almost the only champion of indissolubility was Mr. Gladstone, who, however, gave his opinion under protest as not being relevant to the practical question, and only because the Government had attempted to base upon the

* *Vide supra*, p. 26.

† Hansard, vol. 146, pp. 759 & foll., 1689 & foll., 208 & foll., 2048 & foll. etc., and vol. 147, p. 718 & foll. ; A. Perkins, *Life of Mrs. Norton.*

Scriptures a bill which perpetuated the unjust inequality between husband and wife, while it interfered, in its original form, with the consciences of the clergy as to the re-marrying of divorced persons in Church. " I have no desire," he said from the first, " that the legislation on this subject should be adapted to my views of the Christian doctrine, but to the general wants and wishes of the country." His one concern on the religious aspect of the question was that the Church law should not be touched, and he desired that a civil form of divorce and re-marriage should be provided which did not touch religion at all. A civil form of marriage having already been introduced into the law, the religious aspect of the question was not conclusive, and divorce could and ought to be dealt with from a purely secular point of view. Laws should not be made to square with particular tenets of the Scriptures. " With regard to the great question of the indissolubility of marriage," he said, " let me observe that we have had too much dogmatism." The Gospels were intended to benefit humanity, " not by means of commands and forms in a rigid shape, but rather by the infusion of a new spirit into the precepts of the law." Adultery as the sole ground for divorce was " a most arbitrary rule." There were "many causes for divorce far more fatal to the great obligations of marriage, as disease, idiocy, crime involving imprisonment for life." The *Reformatio Legum*, which had been relied upon by the Government in support of a new and arbitrary interpretation, when there were no less than seven, of the passage in Matthew alone, had, as he pointed out, laid down five or six grounds for divorce besides adultery, such as long-continued strife, and did not violate the "cardinal Christian principle" of the equality of the sexes. He insisted upon the importance of a comparative study of modern legislation upon the subject so that the law might be placed upon the basis of a wide experience instead of upon fashionable opinions which were temporary and local. They ought to "elevate their vision and take less contracted views of the operations of the human mind than they were apt to do, from a defect, he feared, inherent in their natural disposition, a defect which prevented their assuming the existence of anything in heaven or earth except that which chanced to be dreamt of in their philosophy, and which made them imagine that what they knew in their sphere comprehended all in God's universe, and that the notions current among themselves afforded grounds for permanent and durable legislation." He was not moved by the argument that this would be the thin end of the wedge. There was no country in the world which had not wider legal grounds for divorce than those in the bill. There was graver danger that the law which they were about to make would create a prescription in its favour, and once made, would not easily be altered at any future time. He did not consider that his advocacy of a liberal law of divorce was inconsistent with his views upon the theological aspect of the matter, and he was prepared, although he saw that it was hopeless in that Parliament, " to join in the introduction of a complete new category of causes for which divorce should be granted." *

Sir George Grey, the Home Secretary, while refusing to accept any amendment of the bill, said that it was impossible to base legislation upon " ingenious excitations of the human mind upon doubtful passages of the Scriptures." The subject of divorce should not be discussed from high theological grounds, but according to " the dictates of reason, the demands of society, and the feelings of human nature." It was idle to discuss the indissolubility of marriage, for marriage had always been dissoluble. The

* Hansard, vol. 147, p. 383 & foll. ; p. 825 & foll.

experience and authority of the whole human race was opposed to the so-called indissolubility of marriage, whether that opinion and practice were called a tribute to human nature, frailty or weakness.*

It was, however, in the interests of women that strenuous attempts were made by Mr. Gladstone and others to amend the bill in Committee and to extend the narrow ground upon which divorce in it was based. Mr. Drummond, whose high-mindedness in the matter could not be doubted, had, like Mr. Gladstone, given expression to his own peculiar reading of the doctrine of indissolubility, but in Committee he was indefatigable in attempting to improve the lot of women. He said that women had the right to object to the competence of a tribunal composed of Members of Parliament, who judged women " according to their own estimates and for their own purposes." The sufferings of women were like those of the victims of the Inquisition, for those who knew their sufferings were interested in concealing them, while women themselves had no voice in the matter. He reminded the House that when the abolition of slavery was under discussion " not one Indian planter ever gave his vote in

* Hansard, *ibid.*, p. 856 & foll.

favour of the slaves. . . . So it was in the present case, and the members of that House were very much in the position of Turks legislating for the inhabitants of the seraglio." If adultery, as many had contended, in itself dissolved marriage, "how many in that House were married?" He moved an amendment proposing cruelty as a ground for divorce, not only physical cruelty and "the brutal violence of drunken husbands," but "more serious lacerations of the heart which took place in the higher regions of society." He gave some striking examples of cases in which women had been made to suffer the most intense agonies of mind, ending in one case in lunacy and suicide, by the systematic brutality and callous behaviour of degraded husbands, who used their legal authority over the children as an instrument for subjecting their matrimonial victims to a reign of terror.*

Mr. Gladstone from first to last insisted upon "the firm, broad and indestructible basis of the equality of the sexes under the Christian law." Women, he urged, were not only entitled to equality but to more sympathy and protection than men. "A very limited portion of the offences committed by women were due to the

* Hansard, *ibid.*, p. 1587 and foll.

mere influence of the sensual passion." In the vast majority of cases where woman sinned she did so from motives far less impure and less ignoble than those which actuated men : because of an aversion to the husband, which was often founded upon his neglect or cruelty even where there was nothing worse, or because of " an attachment, which, though guilty, was not a gross attachment," for another object. The woman was punished in all cases for a crime which in her case she did not contemplate at the outset, and the penalty therefore could not have a deterring effect. It was idle to talk of the wife seeking protection from her father against the cruelty of her husband. In the right of divorce the wife would have " a sheathed sword which the law put into her hands and which she could at the proper moment draw from the scabbard " and use " in case of extremity." Knowledge was power, and she would have more influence over her husband, who would be deterred from committing " offences which among husbands are infinitely more common than among wives." Cruelty of insult, which " sends the iron into the soul as deeply, and far more sharply, than any material instrument can send it into the body," was as abominable as physical cruelty, which alone the law recognised, and then not as a ground for divorce but as a necessary additional element to the husband's adultery. The law "legalised the husband's adultery" and "put a premium on his adultery by adding either desertion or cruelty to his adultery." He referred to a letter which he had received from a married woman, who said that her husband "openly boasted that the laws of England did not recognise adultery on the part of the husband as a sufficient ground for divorce, and that consequently it was no sin." *

The present English law of divorce was thus condemned by some of the most eminent English statesmen, upholders of the family and of the sanctity of marriage, before it became a blot upon the statute-book. The arguments of Mr. Gladstone and the few who saw the injustice of the law remained unanswered, if they were not unanswerable, refuted the whole episcopal bench, the whole practice of the Canon law, and the laws made by the Reformers, and laid down the principles of modern legislation in divorce. The prediction of Mr. Gladstone has come true: the law has, as he said it would, "created a prescription in its favour" and has established a public opinion and a legal tradition which is always ready to defend the "accidental

* Hansard, *ibid.*, pp. 1272-1274 & foll., 1558 & foll., 1589 & foll.

adulteries " of the husband, and to throw the
stone of opprobrium at the wife, who for any
cause whatever leaves her husband or commits
the only crime which is likely, if her husband is
willing to give her her freedom, to release her from
an intolerable or unhappy marriage.   The same
opinion and tradition condemns her even where
she exercises her legal right of divorce after
enduring the double degradation which the law
compels her to suffer.   As has always happened
when a rigid law is made in the name of religion,
the courts by a gradual process of interpretation
have come to recognise private deeds of separation which are in effect divorces by mutual
consent, while both parties are condemned to
celibacy in theory at least until one of them dies.
The number of such private separations is
incalculable, while the number of divorces
according to the latest statistics is increasing
in spite of and perhaps because of the inherent
injustice of the law.   The policy of the English
law appears to be to encourage private and
judicial separations in which the parties, as Lord
Stowell once said, are left " in the undefined and
dangerous characters of a wife without a husband and a husband without a wife," or, as an
eminent American judge said, " in a situation
where there is an irresistible temptation to the

commission of adultery, unless they possess more frigidity or more virtue than usually falls to the share of human beings." The empty name of marriage, it appears, must be maintained at all costs, and this, as we have seen, is due to the continuance in England of the Catholic Canon law, which has been almost universally condemned by the greatest English thinkers and statesmen. Nor has the mischief been confined to the island of Britain, for the English law and the Canon law which it has everywhere perpetuated, has had a wide influence, as we shall see, in the United States of America and in many of the British colonies. The example of England and the intolerant public opinion which her law of divorce has brought into being pervades in a very great measure the whole of the English-speaking world.*

The English law of divorce was made at a time when the people had very slight representation in Parliament and when the dominating spirit of legislation and of society, the same spirit which until recently refused to pass the Deceased Wife's Sister Bill, was that of the

* Bishop, § 29. See also the remarks of Lord Gorell, then President of the Divorce Court, reported in 1906, L.T. Rep., vol. 94, page 709 and foll., where he speaks of both the highly unsatisfactory character of judicial and magisterial separations "as tending to demoralisation and providing inadequate justice to the innocent," and of the unsatisfactory nature of the English law of divorce and the urgent need of reform.

Established Church, and a society which paid more attention to the plausibilities of life than to liberty and happiness. Perhaps the most striking feature of the debates during the passage of the Divorce Act of 1857 was the reckless absence or suppression of information on the part of those who were responsible for the Act, as to what had been done in other countries. The arguments in defence of the bill or against the passage of any law at all consisted of special pleading by men whose tradition was that of the monks who made the Canon law. Not only were the writings of the greatest minds who had thought upon the subject from Roman times practically unknown, but even the views of Bentham, who had already exercised and was still to exercise an almost unparalleled influence upon legal reform, were either unknown or were ignored, though they had been published in England. It may be useful before closing this chapter to briefly indicate the views of Bentham upon this subject, especially as they are mainly in agreement with those of Mr. Gladstone, who was probably more influenced by his writings than he cared to acknowledge owing to the religious gulf between them.

Bentham, who died in 1832, the year of the first Reform Act, after a long and laborious life spent in advocating, for the time being in vain, a large number of law reforms, many of which have been since carried out, laid down the fundamental principle of legislation that " the public good ought to be the object of legislation." Bentham condemned all attempts to base legislation upon Scriptural texts or upon an ascetic principle, by which man was regarded as " a degenerate being who ought to punish himself without ceasing for the crime of being born." Ecclesiastical history, he said, was " an incontestible proof of the frightful evils which have resulted from religious maxims badly understood." He begins his analysis of the marriage and divorce laws by showing that kings have always been able to obtain divorce and to avoid the blot of incest by " addressing themselves to an experienced chemist, who changed at his pleasure the colour of certain actions." He regards divorce mainly as a protection for women, for while the end of man in the marriage contract might be only " the gratification of a transient passion, and, that passion satisfied, he would have had all the advantages of the union without any of its inconveniences, it was not so with the woman, to whom the engagement had very durable and burdensome consequences." By marriage a woman gave up everything to the man and sacrificed her youth and beauty to him only on this condition, "if I give myself up to you, you shall not be free to leave me without my consent." "But," says Bentham, "what shall we think if the woman adds this clause, 'We shall not be at liberty to separate, though hereafter we come to hate each other as we now love'? Such a condition would seem an act of folly; it has something about it contradictory and absurd which shocks at the first glance: everybody would agree in regarding such a promise as rash, and in thinking that humanity requires it to be omitted. But it is not the woman who asks, it is not the man who invokes this absurd and cruel clause: it is the law which imposes it on both as a condition which cannot be avoided. If there were a law which forbade the taking a partner, a guardian, a manager, a companion, except on the condition of always keeping him, what tyranny, what madness it would be called! Yet a husband is a companion, a guardian, a manager, a partner, and more yet: and still, in the greater part of civilised countries, a husband cannot be had except for life. To live under the perpetual authority of a man you hate, is of itself a state of slavery: but to be compelled to submit to his embraces, is a misfortune too great even for slavery itself. Is it said that the yoke is mutual? That only doubles the misfortune. What more terrible to bear than the indissolubility of this contract? Whether it be a marriage, a country, a condition of any kind, a prohibition to go out of it must operate as a prohibition to enter in. When death is the only deliverer, what horrible temptations, what crimes, may result from a position so fatal! The examples which remain unknown are perhaps more numerous than those that come to light." *

Bentham next examines the various objections to divorce. The parties, it is said, will not regard their lot as irrevocably fixed and there will be perpetual insecurity. He answers that the same inconvenience exists in part under other names during an indissoluble marriage, whenever affection is extinguished. "The strict duties of marriage and its prohibitions so easily eluded, rather serve to produce inconstancy than to prevent it. Render marriage dissoluble, and there would be more apparent separations but fewer real ones." The reciprocal interests of the parties, the children, and common habits of life would all tend to make marriage life-long even if no laws ordained it, and it is only in the

* Bentham, *Theory of Legislation*, III, v, 2 and *passim*.

rare cases where mutual affection is at an end
that the allowance of divorces becomes im-
perative. "But we must look," he says, "to
the advantages of dissolubility. Both parties,
knowing what they might lose, would cultivate
those means of pleasing from which their mutual
affection originated. They would take more
pains to study and to humour each other's
disposition. In one word, care, attention, com-
plaisance would be prolonged after marriage :
and what is now done only to gain affection
would then be practised to preserve it." He
points out that where mutual consent or crime
alone are grounds for divorce there might be
" a disposition to maltreat the feebler party in
order to consent to divorce." Women, therefore,
whose "interests have been neglected too much
in legislation," need more protection than men
by a liberal divorce law.

As to what would become of the children in
case of divorce, he asks, "What would become of
them if death dissolved it ?" In case of divorce
the disadvantage is not so great because "their
education will suffer less than it would have done
from domestic discords and hatred. If the
interests of the children would justify the
prohibition of second marriages in case of divorce,
for a much stronger reason might the same

prohibition be justified in the case of death."
He says that " divorces are not common in
those countries where they have been for a long
time permitted." He strongly condemns judicial separations, of which he says, " The ascetic
principle, hostile to pleasure, has only consented
to the assuagement of suffering. The outraged
woman and her tyrant undergo the same lot :
but this apparent equality covers an inequality
too real. Opinion leaves a great freedom to the
man, while it imposes the strictest restraints
upon the woman." *

The writings of John Stuart Mill, Bentham's
greater disciple, especially his great work on
The Subjection of Women which was published a
year or two after the Divorce Act, ought to be
too well known to need more than the briefest
mention. Although none knew more than he
the bitterness of the divorce law, and no one was
more reticent in proclaiming to the world the
injustice under which he suffered under that law,
here and there he gives us a glimpse of what his
view of that law is, and what marriage might be
if husband and wife were equal. As the wife is
entirely in the power of her husband, " a power
which the clodhopper exercises equally with the
highest nobleman," " it is," he says, " a very

* J. Bentham (1748-1832), *Theory of Legislation.*

cruel aggravation of her fate that she should be allowed to try this chance only once. . . . Since her all in life depends upon obtaining a good master, she should be allowed to change again and again until she finds one. . . . In some slave codes the slave could, under certain circumstances of ill-usage, legally compel the master to sell him, but no amount of ill-usage, without adultery superadded, will in England free a wife from her tormenter." Like Bentham, he bases marriage solely upon the consent and affection of the parties, who ought to be equal in all rights. "What marriage may be," he says, "in the case of two persons of cultivated faculties, identical in opinions and purposes, between whom there exists that best kind of equality, similarity of powers and capacities, with reciprocal superiority in them, so that each can enjoy the luxury of looking up to the other, and can have alternately the pleasure of leading and of being led in the path of development—I will not attempt to describe. To those who can conceive it, there is no need : to those who cannot, it would appear the dream of an enthusiast. But I maintain, with the profoundest conviction, that this, and this only, is the ideal of marriage." This ideal, which is as different as light is from darkness from that so-called holy state in which the parties are legally bound to one another in an indissoluble state of mutual slavery, and in which the woman is in indissoluble subjection to a man, Mill himself realised for a few brief years. In his *Autobiography*, in which he too modestly records a life, which, for its purity and its high and noble aims for the elevation of humanity, has rarely been equalled, and in his recently published *Letters*, we are told in a few words the story of his " incomparable friendship " for Mrs. Taylor, which after twenty years ended in their marriage, by the death of Mr. Taylor, to whom she had been married at a time when, as is the case with many women who are induced to contract a marriage of convenience, she could not know her own mind. For twenty years the outward appearance of a tie which existed only in legal form had to be maintained by her and Mr. Taylor, and she and Mill had to face the taunts and suspicions of friends and relatives alike. During this period she lived, as Mill tells us, mostly in a quiet part of the country with one young daughter, generally apart from her husband, and there Mill visited her and frequently travelled with her, and collaborated with her in his writings. Neither considered the " ordinances of society binding upon a subject so entirely personal," but they were obliged to carefully avoid their conduct in any way bringing discredit upon the husband and therefore upon the wife. Their strength of character enabled them to disregard the criminal interpretation which any modern judge or jury would be only too prone to place upon their intimacy, and, as Mill tells us, their conduct during those years, gave not the slightest ground for any other supposition than the true one, that their " relation to each other at that time was one of strong affection and confidential intimacy only." After the death of the nominal and legal husband, for whom both had the greatest respect, Mill, on his marriage with Mrs. Taylor in 1851, drew up a document in which he renounced all right to control the person, property and freedom of action of his wife, and declared it to be his will, and the condition of their engagement, that she retained in all respects the same absolute freedom of action, and freedom and disposal of herself and of all her property, as if no such marriage had taken place, and he absolutely disclaimed and repudiated " all pretence to have acquired any *rights* by virtue of such marriage."

Such is the history of divorce in England, and an account of what the most eminent Englishmen, of different creeds and philosophies, have thought and endeavoured to do to restore the Anglo-Saxon laws which Archbishop Theodore approved. The list is not long, but it is an honourable one, containing the names of two Lord Chancellors, one of whom was a Catholic, the first Protestant Archbishop of Canterbury, John Milton, John Selden, Bentham, John Stuart Mill, and the late Mr. Gladstone, one of Britain's most eminent Churchmen and statesmen. Although the Canon law has gained the victory by the law of prescription, the verdict of history must be given to those who lost ; who were " like one who goes by night, and carries the light behind him, and profits not himself, but makes others wise that follow him." *

* Dante, Purg., 22, 67-9.

X

THE UNITED STATES OF AMERICA

" As it is impossible to harmonise the conflicting religious views by legislation, the legislatures of this country must act upon the subject in respect solely of its political and social bearings, and if they establish laws permitting divorce, they do not therefore injure, even in the inmost conscience, those who deem marriage a religious sacrament and indissoluble. Such persons are under no compulsion to use the divorce laws, by appearing as plaintiff in divorce suits, and, if they are made defendants, having violated their matrimonial duties civilly, they cannot complain of being cut off from their matrimonial rights civilly."

BISHOP, " Marriage and Divorce," § 32.

THESE words of one of the greatest American authorities on divorce, represent the fundamental principle of divorce in America. [The influence of the English law, however, especially the decisions of the English ecclesiastical courts, has been very great in America, not only in the definition of the grounds for divorce, but in establishing many of the restrictions and inequalities of the Canon-law.

The colonists who founded the various States from the time of Elizabeth took with them the common law of England, but, being Protestants and having no Established Church or episcopal courts, the ecclesiastical or Canon law of England was not followed. Marriage was a civil contract usually entered into before a magistrate. By the Puritan legislation of New England the right of divorce was recognised but was rarely exercised. The attitude of the Puritans towards the Canon law may be expressed in the words of the American historian, "Divorce from bed and board, the separate maintenance without the dissolution of the marriage contract—an anomaly in Protestant legislation, that punishes the innocent more than the guilty—was utterly abhorrent from their principles." Divorce from the earliest times was granted by the governors in council, and, as the legislatures took the place of these, the practice of divorce by private statute was gradually established as in England, whose example was followed, although the practice in America was not so cumbrous or so expensive as in England. In New York only four divorces appear to have been granted before the Revolution, these being granted by the Governor in Council at an early date. "This strictness," says Justice Kent, "was productive of public inconvenience and often forced the parties, in cases which rendered a separation fit and necessary, to some other State, to avail themselves of a more easy and certain remedy"; words which are prophetic of a condition of things not unknown in some of the American and other modern States at the present day. Adultery, following the English practice, appears to have been the principal ground for divorce, and in many of the colonies desertion, cruelty and impotence, while husband and wife were generally equal.*

After the United States had obtained her independence in 1782, divorce by private statute continued in practice for more than half a century in the majority of the State legislatures, in whom exclusive power over divorce was vested by the American Constitution. Gradually, however, the grounds for divorce began to be defined by their legislatures, and the ordinary law courts or the courts of chancery were granted jurisdiction. Georgia, Mississippi and Alabama were the first to abolish legislative divorces, though the sanction of a two-thirds majority was still required after the court had pronounced a decree. In the other States, however, legislative divorces were employed, where there were defects in the general divorce laws, until about the middle of the nineteenth century, when in

---

* Bancroft, *History of the United States* (15th ed.), I, p. 465 ; Bishop, §§ 71-77, 663-685 ; Kent, *Commentaries*, II, p. 97 and foll. ; Howard, *History of Matrimonial Institutions*, vol. II, p. 330, and vol. III, p. 3.

the majority of States this kind of divorce was abolished by them. Legislative divorce, however, is still practised in Connecticut.*

The grounds for divorce at present vary considerably in the different States, the principal ones being adultery, cruelty, desertion, insanity and other serious diseases or incapacities, such as impotence, habitual drunkenness ; grounds denoting an irreconcilable difference between the parties, such as long absence, refusal to fulfil marital duties, gross misbehaviour repugnant to the marriage contract and violent and ungovernable temper. In some States divorce has been left entirely to the discretion of the judges, where this appears to be conducive to domestic harmony and consistent with the peace and morality of society. Incompatibility of temper, or invincible aversion between the parties, though not expressly recognised, is in practice the deciding element in most cases, and generally the welfare of the parties is considered, although their wishes are as a rule disregarded where they are known.†

* See *U.S.A. Constitutions, passim ; Special Acts and Resolutions of the State of Connecticut*, vol. 14, pp. 706 and 855.

† Burge (2nd ed.), III, pp. 892-6 ; Bishop, §§ 771, 815-27 and *passim* ; Bouvier, *Law Dictionary of United States* (ed., Rawle), *s.v.* "Divorce" ; *Reports on the Laws of Marriage and Divorce* (1894), part 2, pp. 157 and foll. See also Hirsh's *Tabulated Digest of the Divorce Laws, in U.S.* (1888-1901).

UNITED STATES OF AMERICA

The divorce laws of America are generally those of the Reformation as extended by judicial interpretation. If there is not some disease or incapacity there must as a rule be some unlawful or disgraceful act on the part of one of the spouses entitling the other to dissolve the marriage. Although marriage is in America, as in all other parts of the civilised world, legally a contract and all attempts to follow the Scriptures appear to have been repudiated, the contract has been deprived of one of its essential elements, until it is generally spoken of by legal authorities as either a " relation " or a " natural right " or as something more than a contract, although that something is certainly not religious. Bishop, who strongly repudiates all attempts to apply dogma to marriage, attempts to explain this anomaly by saying that the public and the children have an interest in all marriages even where the parties cannot and do not live together, and he thinks that judges ought always to be extremely careful before granting divorces. How the public can have an interest in maintaining a marriage which exists only in name and where there can be no prejudice to the rights of third parties, it is difficult to conceive. Bishop admits that " children born during a discordant cohabitation have their natures

215

tainted by it; while their education, in which also the State has the highest interest, will not be of a salutary character." It is, however, not the interest of the public or of the children which underlies the divorce laws of America, in which the wishes of the parties who alone have to bear the brunt of it are ignored, but the dogmatic conception common to Reformers and Canonists alike, that the judge represents the Deity in separating those "whom God has joined" and a desire to conform in some way to the indissolubility of marriage.*

There is no doubt that the Canon law in one or other of its various forms has been followed to a very large extent by the judges in interpreting the law. Bishop asserts the astounding doctrine that the ecclesiastical law, which he considered was part of the common law of England, lay dormant in America for two centuries because there were no courts which were competent to administer it, and that when, after the Revolution, courts were established with jurisdiction over divorce, the ecclesiastical law awoke from its long sleep and the courts became entitled to administer it. This doctrine expresses the practice of many of the States, and has only been expressly repudiated by judicial decision

* Bishop, §§ 33-37, 41.

216

a year or two ago. It is now law that the ecclesiastical law of England never formed part of the common law which was taken over by America. But the judges who laid down the practice from the time of the Revolution followed the practice of the English ecclesiastical courts, and many of the rules of the Canon law, such as judicial separation, nullity of marriage, the preference of the rights of the husband over those of the wife, especially in defining cruelty to mean danger to life or limb, in fact all the English practice except the restitution of conjugal rights, have been incorporated by judicial interpretation into the American practice, generally without any legislative authority whatever. The divorce law of America, in fact, is more a judge-made law than that of any other country, and the unwarranted adoption of a great part of the Canon law in America can only be paralleled by that of the judges of most Protestant States immediately after the Reformation in following the same law, which the Reformation had expressly repudiated.*

The people who drafted the original divorce laws certainly had no intention of introducing the Canon law or the ecclesiastical laws of the

* Bishop, §§ 71-77 ; *Journal of the Society of Comparative Legislation,* vol. XIX, N.S., August, 1908, p. 188.

country from which they had recently obtained their liberty by force of arms. The judges, however, who in America have probably more power than in any country in the world, owing to the constitutional separation of the judicial, executive and legislative powers, thought otherwise. As Bishop says, "The statutory law of this country upon this subject seems in general to have been drafted by men who either did not possess much knowledge of the unwritten laws respecting it, or did not regard such unwritten laws as worthy to be considered in framing the statutes." Thus we find the judges soon interpreting the statutes in accordance with what they considered to be the " unwritten law," a law which has only recently been declared to be non-existent, and relying in their decisions upon the English ecclesiastical law, the Canon law, passages from the Bible, and from the English Book of Common Prayer. Thus collusion, connivance and recrimination have been adopted by the courts to deprive both parties of divorce. Sometimes, as Bishop tells us, " a statute has been frittered away by judges who seemed to regard it as part of their calling to cast every obstruction in the path of parties seeking this remedy.*

* Bishop, §§ 47, 87-9 and foll.

218

UNITED STATES OF AMERICA

The peculiar feature of the American law of divorce, in effect, is the wide discretion which the judges have been allowed to exercise. Although this is a dangerous discretion, and its existence is solely due to historical causes, there seems to be no reason why a judge, if allowed to exercise a discretion at all, should only be allowed to exercise it in refusing divorce, but should have an equal discretion, as in some of the American States, such as Maine, Iowa, North Carolina and Connecticut, to allow it even where there does not appear to be any illegal act or impediment on the part of one of the spouses. Morality and society are not likely to suffer by allowing each party to contract a fresh marriage should they desire it.

Bishop says of the practice of Connecticut that, notwithstanding the liberty of divorce, or in consequence of it, there is no State in the Union in which domestic felicity and purity, unblemished morals and matrimonial concord and virtue more abound than in Connecticut. If this discretion is in some cases " exceedingly embarrassing and painful in the exercise to the judges," the necessity of having to undergo a public and minute inquiry into the secrets of family life is as embarrassing and painful to judges and to the parties themselves in all cases. As Bishop says, "Perfect uniformity of decision, desirable as it is, cannot be expected upon this subject. Judges are men; men are fallible; fallible men see things differently." The truth is that the public inquiry into divorce cases and the exercise of judicial discretion are the *damnosa hereditas* of the Canon law, and modern judges in America as well as in all other countries where the grounds for divorce are inquired into, are the legal successors of the bishops who administered that law.*

No one more than Bishop has condemned the indissolubility of marriage and judicial separation. Of the latter he says that it is " made up of pious doctrine and worldly stupidity " and is " the most corrupting device ever imposed upon a blind and pliant community." Of the former he says that those who imagine that the feelings of the parties are of no concern, and that marriage means the mere compulsory living together in the same house, " are permitted, for all the author cares, to turn up their prude faces and talk of corruption . . . but never will their debasing rule of rusty iron be allowed to restrain the uprising of the better instincts of the people of this country who . . . are bringing marriage both in law and practice into the condition which

* Bishop, §§ 26 and note, 41, 753, 826-7.

the Maker intended." He condemns the idea of the parties placing themselves in each other's power for life so as to be incapable of freeing themselves by any act of the law, though the ends of their union are all frustrated, though one of them is unworthy to discharge the duties undertaken, though every hope of its ministering to the well-being of the parties is obliterated." "The truth is," he says, "that either divorces or illicit connections will prevail in every community, and it is for the legislature to choose between the two." He cites the opinion of an eminent American judge who said, "It is a great hardship that a person, who has been unfortunate in forming a matrimonial connection, must be for ever precluded from any possibility of extricating himself from such a misfortune and be shut out from enjoying the best pleasures of life. This consideration, instead of adding to happiness of the connection, must frighten persons from entering into it. It is therefore the best policy to admit a dissolution of the contract when it is evident that the parties cannot derive from it the benefits for which it was instituted ; and when, instead of being a source of the highest pleasure and most enduring felicity, it becomes a source of the deepest woe and misery." Bishop considers that there is no danger in increasing the facilities for divorce and no fear of people rushing heedlessly into marriage and being careless of their conduct afterwards if divorce is freely allowed.*

In South Carolina there is no divorce law, and it was said by one of its judges that in "South Carolina, to her unfading honour, a divorce has not been granted since the Revolution." Bishop cites a case in which "a man took his negro slave-woman to his bed and table and compelled the unoffending wife to receive the crumbs after her," and the State to its unfading honour refused any remedy to the wife. "In this country," said one judge of that State in a certain case, "where divorces are not allowed for any cause whatever, we sometimes see men of excellent characters unfortunate in their marriages, and virtuous women abandoned or driven away houseless by their husbands, who would be doomed to celibacy and solitude if they did not form connections which the law does not allow, and who *make excellent husbands and virtuous wives* still. Yet they are considered as living in adultery because a rigorous and unyielding law, from motives of policy alone, has ordained it so." †

* Bishop, §§ 29, 32-37, 44.
† Bishop, §§ 38, 42. By a law of 1868, provision was made in the constitution of South Carolina for a divorce law, but none has been made. (See *Federal and State Constitutions*.)

Bishop warns us that as we derive all our laws of divorce from Catholic ecclesiastics " who held to the indissolubility of marriage as a point of religious belief, it is not strange that much of our legal literature upon this subject has the hue which such a belief imports." It is to be feared that Bishop, like Brouwer, whom he freely quotes, was not altogether free from this " hue," for he is in spite of himself imbued with the ecclesiastical laws which he so freely criticises. He approves and defends the divorce law of the French Revolution, but ignores its example. He appears also to follow the obsolete conception of the Law of Nature, and can only think of divorce in America as the object of a minute judicial inquiry, and wherever the causes of divorce are not capable of the exact definition required by an indictment such as some overt and generally some criminal act, he regards the ground for divorce as " uncertain and shadowy." He says of cases in which there is an " undefinable jarring of natures coming into collision, and other mental causes which render the marriage burdensome," that these " are of a subtle nature and human tribunals cannot well deal with them." Divorce in his view is, in fact, nothing else than a branch of the criminal law.*

* Bishop, §§ 41-44.

223   Q

A HISTORY OF DIVORCE

Some of the restrictions against one of the spouses being allowed to re-marry after divorce were taken over by the legislatures of some of the States, but they have with a few exceptions been abolished. In some States there is a tendency to protect women and children by allowing the wife a separate domicil and by recognising children born of a bigamous marriage or an adulterous connection as being legitimate. The laws of America may be said to be generally tending towards allowing divorce in all cases where it appears that the parties are irreconcilable. Husband and wife are in all States on the same footing in the divorce law.*

While the authority of Bishop may be taken for the fact that where the law of divorce is liberal, marriage and morality are in a healthy condition, recent writers, such as Mr. Bryce, say that " there seems to be no ground for concluding that the increase of divorce in America necessarily points to a decline in the standard of domestic morality, and the same conclusion may well be true regarding the greater frequency of divorce all over the world." †

* Burge (1910), III, p. 896; Bishop, §§ 301-319.

† Bryce, *Studies in History and Jurisprudence*, II, p. 463, &c., also in the new edition of his *American Commonwealth*; *Encyclopædia Britannica*, 11th ed., *sub voce* Divorce; Münsterberg, *The Americans* (transl. by Holt), pp. 523, 575.

XI

THE BRITISH COLONIES

" Until the present generation she [England] has been
on the same bad level with other countries as to the
amount of self-government which she allowed them [the
Colonies] to exercise through the representative institutions
that she conceded to them. She claimed to be arbiter
even of their purely internal concerns, according to her
own, not their ideas, of how those concerns could be best
regulated."—JOHN STUART MILL

(Representative Government).

" Since 1899 the imperial power of disallowing Colonial
Acts has not been exercised except in the case of Acts that
clashed with imperial interests."

CAMBRIDGE MODERN HISTORY, XII, p. 649.

IN the three ancient kingdoms which now
form the United Kingdom three entirely
different divorce laws are in force. In
Ireland divorce is only obtainable by a private
Act of the Imperial Parliament after a judicial
separation has been obtained in the Supreme
Court of Ireland ; in Scotland either party may
obtain a divorce on the ground of desertion or
adultery ; in England divorce is only obtainable on the ground of adultery, with the necessity, where the wife is plaintiff, of proving

227

some additional offence, which is in itself in other countries a sufficient ground for divorce. An even wider diversity of laws exists throughout the rest of the British Empire. In addition to these or similar laws, other laws of divorce are in force in some of the colonies, such as the Roman-Dutch law and the French law as it was at some period of its history, while in the Eastern portions of the Empire divorce by mutual consent is recognised where the parties profess certain religious beliefs. In other parts of the Empire there is no divorce law at all, or no tribunal with jurisdiction over divorce.*

The reason for this diversity is purely historical. In the colonies of British origin the colonists took with them the English law as it happened to be at the time of the foundation of the various colonies, and this law has remained, or the law of England at some period of its history has been proclaimed to be in force. The early Governors and legislative bodies were not allowed to pass laws which were repugnant to the law of England. Early in the nineteenth century it became the rule to insert in the Governor's commission a clause saying that he was " not to give his assent to any bill that may be passed by the council and assembly . . . for

* Burge, 2nd ed., pp. 856, 877, and Ch. XVI and *passim*.

the divorce of persons joined together in holy matrimony." This clause was inserted in the commission of the Governor of Ceylon in 1831, of Newfoundland in 1832, and of Jamaica about the same time. It was also inserted in the commissions of the Governors-General of Canada until 1878, when it was discontinued owing to strong representations made by the then Minister of Justice that such a power was in conflict with the constitutional privileges of the Dominion. In the other colonies, however, divorce legislation continued to be reserved by the Governors in accordance with their commissions until quite recently, having been exercised in the case of New Zealand as late as 1907.[*]

In the colony of the Straits Settlements, which obtained its law in 1807, the English ecclesiastical laws are administered by the local Supreme Court, " as far as circumstances will permit," and only judicial separations and declarations of nullity are therefore recognised. In the Channel Islands, where the English Divorce Acts do not apply, either judicial separation or no remedy at all is obtainable, the practice varying in the

---

[*] Stokes, p. 14 and pp. 149-150 ; Gemmill (prefatory note by Bourinot) ; Clark ,p. 573 (Ceylon), p. 347 (Jamaica), p. 439 (Newfoundland). Newfoundland seems to be the only self-governing colony where there is no law of divorce ; (See Burge, 2nd ed., I, p. 234, and III, p. 881) ; New Zealand, Act 78 of 1907.

different islands. In the Isle of Man the practice is similar to that of England before the Divorce Act of 1857, and a judicial separation in the local court has to be followed by a private divorce Act in the local Parliament. In Trinidad, Tobago, Hong Kong and Zanzibar, the local Supreme Courts have no divorce jurisdiction, while in British Honduras the Supreme Court has jurisdiction, but has no divorce law to administer. In some Crown colonies there is only judicial separation,* while in others the English Divorce Act has been proclaimed and is administered by the local courts.† In the colonies of Uganda, Nyasaland and British East and West Africa, a law based upon the English Act has been put into force, but the jurisdiction of the local courts has been restricted to cases in which either the marriage or the matrimonial offence has taken place in those parts. Colonists in all these parts of the Empire, as they have ceased to reside in the United Kingdom, have by colonisation in effect lost their national right of divorce in the place of their origin, and, where the local laws do not admit of divorce, or only in circumstances which

* *E.g.* Barbadoes, Grenada and St. Vincent.

† *E.g.* Bahama Islands, Jamaica, Falkland Islands, St. Helena, Fiji and Cyprus.

may not cover their particular cases, it does not appear that they can obtain divorce at all except possibly by a Special Act of the Imperial Parliament or by abandoning their domicil or nationality. The dominating spirit of all the divorce legislation which Britain has granted to the Crown colonies is that of the Canon law, with its fictions of the indissolubility of marriage and of the absolute indentity of husband and wife, the husband being regarded as the " head."*

The colonies and dominions of British origin which enjoy responsible government commenced, like America and the Crown colonies, with the English law and all its ecclesiastical anomalies. In Canada the law has been allowed to remain for the most part as it was. By the British North America Act of 1867 the Dominion Parliament obtained the sole right of legislation in divorce, and, instead of passing a general Divorce Act, the laws which were in force in the various provinces have been allowed to remain, while no fewer than a hundred and forty private Divorce Acts dealing with individual cases have been passed since 1867 by the Dominion Parliament. The life-senators, following the ancient and illustrious example of the spiritual and temporal peers in England, inquire into all

* Burge, 2nd ed., I, 193, and III, 889-890 ; III, 878-892 and *passim.*

cases where a private Act is sought, and, after long delay, political exigencies and considerable expense to the parties, divorce is granted on the ground of adultery alone, although there is no law restricting divorce to that ground, and no distinction is made in practice between the rights of husband and wife. In those provinces which had either not passed or received a general law of divorce before confederation, and in all new provinces, it is necessary for the parties to apply to the Dominion Parliament for divorce.* In these provinces there is no court with jurisdiction over divorce, though the Supreme Court dissolves marriage as a civil contract, where there is some Canonistic defect or impediment, under the fiction that the marriage has never taken place. In Prince Edward Island the Lieutenant-Governor was in 1836 granted jurisdiction over divorce where there was impotence, adultery or relationship, with power to delegate his jurisdiction to the Chief Justice. This power, however, remains " dormant," together with the right of divorce. In Nova Scotia, New Brunswick and British Columbia the English Divorce Act was proclaimed before confederation, but the rights

* *Viz.*, Ontario, Quebec (Canon law), Manitoba and the N.W. Territories.

of husband and wife have been equalised in the
first two, while in Nova Scotia cruelty has been
made an additional ground for divorce.* Why
the Canadian Parliament has not thought it
desirable, as a Canadian judge said, " to elevate a
moral right to legislative favour into a legal
right enforceable by statute," is undoubtedly due
to Catholic influence, which has, even from the
time of the union of Upper and Lower Canada
in 1792, placed every obstacle in the way both
of individual divorces and of any attempt to
amend the laws, even though the Imperial
Government in 1869 suggested that a law on the
lines of the English Divorce Act should be
made.†

In Australia and New Zealand the English
Divorce Act was put into force between 1860 and
1873, and has in those dominions always operated
as a strong vested interest against all attempts to
introduce a more liberal and equable law. Even
after the granting of responsible government,
these colonies have had to contend with the
Imperial veto. As Mr. Dicey tells us, " Acts

* Cruelty was substituted for desertion by 1 Geo. III, cap. 17 (N.S.),
in order, as the Act states, to make it more in conformity with the
English law.

† Burge, 2nd ed., III, pp. 878-881 ; Watts v. Watts, [1908], A.C. 573 ;
Gemmill, prefatory note and pp. 16-43, *et passim* ; Bourinot, pp. 796-
800 ; Wheeler, pp. 249-253. A great number of Canadians cross over
into the United States in order to obtain divorces.

passed by colonial legislatures allowing divorce on the ground of the husband's adultery and legalising marriage with a deceased wife's sister have been disallowed by the home Government." In Victoria it is still necessary for a wife who sues for a divorce on the ground of her husband's adultery to prove that it took place "within the conjugal residence or coupled with circumstances or conduct of aggravation or of a repeated adultery." While the English law remains in force in the other colonies of Australia, in New South Wales, Victoria and New Zealand important amendments have been made by the local legislatures from the year 1890. In these colonies husband and wife have been placed on an equal footing (with the exception of adultery in Victoria), and besides adultery, desertion, habitual drunkenness and conviction for serious crimes are grounds for divorce. In New Zealand insanity and the murder or attempted murder of one of the children by either of the spouses are additional grounds. In all these colonies, however, the English grounds for divorce have been retained as additional grounds, but it is clear that they are now little more than pious verbiage. The practice of the courts has always closely followed that of the old English ecclesiastical courts, *i.e.*, the Canon law, and its principal rules are still recognised as binding.*

The greater part of the British Empire, however, is governed by divorce laws of entirely different origin, which have been generally, as a concession to the original inhabitants upon annexation, allowed to remain in force. In Trinidad the Spanish law was allowed to remain at the time of the conquest in 1797, so there is no divorce in that island. In Mauritius the Code Napoléon was expressly maintained when that colony was ceded to Great Britain in 1810, and remained in force until 1872, when divorce by mutual consent was abolished by the British Government at a time when there was no representative government on that island, and in its place desertion and long absence were added to the Civil Code as grounds for divorce, and husband and wife put upon an equal footing. The judges, as a learned authority states, frequently attempt to reconcile the parties before leave to sue is given. " Reconciliations are seldom effected, but there have been cases in which the judge has insisted on a postponement of the proceedings in order to

---

* Dicey, *Law of the Constitution*, 3rd ed., p. 111 ; in New South Wales Acts of 1877, 1879 and 1881 were disallowed ; Burge, 2nd ed., III, 881-6, and see the *Statutes* of the various Colonies.

give the parties time for reflection." The same
paternal solicitude on the part of the judges is
in vogue in St. Lucia, which was annexed in 1814,
and appears to have suffered by the Catholic
reaction in France, for there divorce is not
allowed, but only judicial separation on the
grounds laid down by the Code Napoléon.
Whenever such separations are refused, cohabitation appears to be enforced by the court,
for "the common life" must be resumed within
the time fixed by the court. In Malta the
same law is in force.*

In the Union of South Africa, Southern Rho-
desia, Ceylon and British Guiana, the Roman-
Dutch law, or the law of Holland as it was at the
beginning of the nineteenth century, is still in
force, and adultery and malicious desertion, the
Scriptural grounds fixed by the Reformers, are
the principal grounds for divorce. Southern Rho-
desia, though a colony of British origin and race,
obtained its law from the Cape Colony. The law
of these colonies has not been codified or even
appreciably modified by legislation, and remains
for the most part as it was fixed by the Reformers,
except where it has been moulded and extended
by judicial interpretation to meet the needs of

* Burge, 2nd ed., I, pp. 199-210, III ; 887-890 ; Clark, *Summary of
Colonial Law*, p. 23.

modern society, an interpretation in which the principles of the Roman law have played their part. Thus, in South Africa the condemnation of one of the spouses to capital punishment where the sentence has been commuted to one of imprisonment for life has been held to be a valid ground for divorce, even though such a sentence is rarely carried out to its full extent. Lord De Villiers, in giving judgment in one case, said:—"A wife who is truly attached to her husband would probably be strengthened in her attachment by misfortunes, which overtake him, even by his own fault, and would be content to remain his wife in the hope that the clemency of the Crown may still enable them to live together as husband and wife. If, however, she has lost her affection for him, it is too much to expect of her that she will continue to be the wife of a man sentenced to imprisonment for life in the vague belief that the clemency of the Crown may some day restore to her the society of the husband whom she has no desire to live with." By divorce the parties are placed in practically the same position as they were in before marriage, husband and wife being equal as regards the remedy of divorce except in the matter of domicil, where the Canon law is still followed, but the grounds for divorce, though no

longer punished as criminal, retain something of
their criminal origin in the fact that the guilty
party is punished as a rule by losing the custody
of the children, though this is a matter largely
in the discretion of the court. The judges do
not always follow the humane opinion of Van
Leeuwen·that " the mother's claim to bring up
the children is the stronger, because a mother's
love conquers all other affections," and it is the
woman who suffers most by the criminal taint
which the old ecclesiastical laws attached to
divorce. *

Desertion in South Africa, though still piously
called " malicious," can no longer be regarded
as such, and the statutory penalty of banishment
which the Reformers laid down has never been
enforced in South Africa, though, like the forbidding of intermarriage between those who
have committed adultery, it still remains for a
memorial on the statute book. No period for
desertion has been fixed in South Africa except
in Natal, where by an Act passed in 1883 before
responsible government was granted, eighteen
months was fixed, and the practice of decrees *nisi*
and the intervention of the Crown Prosecutor in
cases of collusion was instituted. In all the other

* Jooste *v.* Jooste, 24 S.C. 329. It is worthy of note that Clark
says (p. 475) that in 1834 the Resident Magistrates and Clerks of
the Peace had jurisdiction over divorce in the country districts.

provinces there need be only clear evidence of immediate and determined desertion, refusal to live with the other party as husband or wife, even while the parties are still living under the same roof for appearance sake, or refusal by the husband to support his wife coupled with absence from her.*

In 1855 an attempt was made in one case by an eminent Scottish judge in the Cape Colony to introduce an arbitrary period for desertion as in the law of Scotland. The learned judge, as the report says, " proceeded to discuss Scriptural authority upon the law of marriage, with reference to Mosaic authority and morality in general "—probably the only case in which Scripture has ever been quoted as a legal authority in a South African court. The same judge, though not calling marriage a sacrament, said that it was "not an ordinary but an extraordinary civil contract regulated by Divine command and put by human law beyond the control of the parties," and was " indissoluble as far as may be." He admitted that marriage, if a contract, was capable of dissolution at the will of the parties like any other contract. He insisted, however, upon the parties endeavouring

* Van Leeuwen, *Censura Forensis*, 1, 1, 15, 16 ; Van Zijl's *Judicial Practice*, 2nd ed., ch. XXIX ; Brown *v.* Brown (1905), T.S. 415 ; Woods *v.* Woods (1907), T.S. 21.

to become reconciled by every possible way before advantage was taken of divorce, and would have dismissed the action, leaving the parties as they were. In that case the absence of the defendant had only been eight days, but the majority of the court refused to listen to the Scriptural and moral advice of Mr. Justice Bell, and being satisfied that the evidence of desertion was clear, and that it was wilful, held that time was not a necessary ingredient in the action.*

More recently, in 1906, the judges in the Transvaal in certain *obiter dicta* in one case suggested that some period for desertion might be fixed by statute, mainly with a view, as they said, of putting a stop to collusion. As one of the judges said, the fixed determination to desert might have been arranged between the parties who both desired the divorce, and " the injured spouse may even be suing at the desire of the guilty party and with the unselfish purpose of setting him free." The same learned judge, however, admitted that even if a period were fixed " collusion would still be possible," and " must from the very nature of the case be very difficult to detect." The avowed reasons of the judges in that case were " to discourage actions for divorce on the ground of desertion when

* 2 Searle's *S.C. Reports*, 128.

some hope of reconciliation remained." No such arbitrary period has, however, been fixed, nor does the fixing of such a period seem desirable, for the parties are usually in the best position to know whether there is hope of reconciliation or not without either paternal advice from the bench or being obliged to wait in a condition of enforced celibacy for a fixed time. It is as a rule not the actual period of desertion that matters, but the long unhappiness and frequently mere formal cohabitation for many years previous. Both parties may have deserted each other either against each other's will or by consent long before the publicity of the divorce court is sought, and frequently it is the one who happens to sue first who is entitled to be considered the innocent party.*

Divorce on the ground of desertion in South Africa must be preceded by an action for the restitution of conjugal rights, as it is called, although the courts have no power to enforce such an order. The order for restitution is " a fictitious preliminary to the action for divorce, for no one would sue a malicious deserter to return if the object was not divorce." As Blackstone says, it is only asked for " if either party be weak

* Krantz *v.* Krantz (1906) T.S. 750 ; Van Leeuwen, *Censura Forensis*, 1, 1, 15, 12.

241

enough to desire it." Some of the South
African courts have expressly laid down that
the action for restitution is merely a formal
condition precedent to a divorce for desertion,
and have granted the order even where the
plaintiff frankly admitted, in answer to the
court, that divorce was his real object and that
he did not wish his wife to return to him.
The decisions on this point have not been uni-
form, and on one occasion a plaintiff, who was
candid enough to answer that he would not
receive his wife, who had deserted him, even if
she came back, and that his real object was
divorce on the ground of desertion, was refused
his remedy. These inquiries into the " mental
attitude " of the plaintiff in the event of something which may but probably will not arise at
a future date are purely speculative, and the
difficulties which such inquiries create are usually
brought about by the judges themselves in their
no doubt laudable desire to see whether there is
any hope of reconciliation, thereby carrying out
the advice to judges of the Synod of Dordrecht
in 1578. Should the plaintiff, when the occasion
arises, not receive the defendant, the latter
would have an action for divorce on the ground
of his malicious desertion. If divorce were
refused because of a hypothetical state of mind,

the result would be, as Sir John Wessels remarked in another case, " that plaintiffs who spoke the truth would fail in their actions and that those who were content to feign a desire which they were far from feeling would succeed," and that " perjury and trickery " would thereby be encouraged. It is by no means clear that the order for restitution, which is unknown in America, was always a necessary preliminary to divorce for desertion in Holland, while it is clear that " the object aimed at in all cases is divorce." The refusal to return after an order of court is merely conclusive proof of desertion, but there can be evidence equally conclusive without the retention of this survival of a state of law which no longer exists and without the fixing of an arbitrary period of desertion.*

Judicial separations and declarations of nullity on the canonical and other grounds have been retained in the Roman-Dutch law, and, although the courts used to insist upon a full inquiry into the causes of separation, the practice of confirming deeds of separation where the parties agree to a separation has become established, but where the parties cannot agree the courts make a full

* Gibbon v. Gibbon, 2 E.D.C., 280 ; Joubert v. Joubert (1902), T.H., 140 ; Venter v. Venter (1903), T.H. 381 ; Krantz v. Krantz (1906), T.S. 750 ; Jooste v. Jooste (1907), 24 S.C. 329, at p. 332 ; Bishop, § 771 ; Blackstone, 15th ed., II, p. 94 ; Brouwer, II, 18.

inquiry into the respective merits of the parties, and actions for separation, like actions for divorce, frequently resolve themselves into mutual incriminations in a public court for the purpose of obtaining the principal or exclusive custody of the children, and into quarrels about the property. Judicial separations as a rule are only requested where no legal ground for divorce exists, but where the parties are irreconcilable. Such separations are in effect divorces, with all the public scandal attaching to divorce, and without the right of either party to re-marry. These actions are, as we have seen, solely survivals of the Canon law.

Another survival of the Canon law which was adopted by the lawyers of the Reformation period, and which still creates considerable difficulty for parties who wish to be divorced, is the doctrine of collusion with its attendant doctrines of recrimination, connivance and condonation. Where one of the parties assists the other to obtain a divorce which both desire, the courts have been known to refuse the divorce and to leave the parties in an equivocal and dangerous condition. In one case in the Transvaal, in 1878, where a wife had committed adultery and was living with another man, the court refused a divorce to the husband solely because he had proposed that the wife should marry the other man, who was apparently poor, and he had promised to contribute to the maintenance of his wife during her second marriage. The principle of such cases appears to be that generosity on the part of the innocent spouse is punished, while he or she is expected to show a greater vindictiveness than is shown by a prosecutor in a criminal case. Connivance and recrimination appear to apply only to adultery and not to desertion. Thus in one case it was held that the fact that a husband had utterly abandoned his wife and left her without means for many years, "so long, indeed, that she represented herself as a widow and had married again," did not prevent the husband from obtaining a divorce on the ground of her "adultery." Mr. Justice Bell in that case doubted whether divorce should be granted, and he was prepared to create a precedent on the ground of "morality and public policy," but he did not explain how morality and public policy would benefit. In that case it is interesting to notice that the judgments of the English ecclesiastical courts were largely cited by the judges, although it is obvious that judgments referring to a system which declared marriage to be dissoluble were no more applicable to divorce under the Roman-Dutch law than the Roman law, as the present Chief Justice remarked in another case, is applicable to judicial separation, which was unknown to it. Condonation or forgiveness still operates frequently to prevent a wife from obtaining a divorce because of an offence which she has forgiven, even where the husband is afterwards guilty of cruelty to her and she wishes to obtain a divorce. In such cases the wife has to be content with a judicial separation, solely on account of her previous generosity or weakness.*

The difficulties of the Roman-Dutch law of divorce, as practised in the various colonies where that law prevails, are mainly caused by the survivals in that law of obsolete dogmas which are no longer considered to be of any practical weight in the decision of cases. Malicious desertion has lost its dogmatic and criminal sting and is no longer malicious except in name. So long as there is a technical ground for divorce by one of the parties finally leaving the other, the parties are now allowed in practice to make arrangements as to the division of the property and the custody of the children, and on these

---

* Weatherly *v.* Weatherly (1878), K., p. 66 ; Farmer *v.* Farmer, 1 S. 227 ; Hasler *v.* Hasler, 13 S.C. 377 ; Weyers *v.* Stopforth, 1 M. 273 ; Dawson *v.* Dawson, 9 S.C. 446 ; Wessels *v.* Wessels, 12 S.C. 465.

matters judgment has been known to be given by consent. The difficulties which still confront both parties are generally more to the disadvantage of the wife than of the husband, for she is in the anomalous position of being a minor subject to his control both as to her person and even her separate property, and only becomes of age and acquires a legal personality when she sues or is sued for divorce or judicial separation. Her domicil being that of her husband, difficulties are often placed in the way of her obtaining a divorce because of this canonistic doctrine, and though the courts endeavour as far as possible to alleviate the lot of women in such cases where the husband is clearly to blame, the doctrine of indentity of domicil has been so strongly established by past judges in all countries, that it appears that nothing short of legislation establishing in all legal rights the independence of the wife, and especially her independent domicile, can bring the present law into conformity with modern ideas. With regard to divorce generally in South Africa, and especially the working of desertion as a ground for divorce, the present Chief Justice, Lord de Villiers, in an article written shortly after the late war, in answer to a proposal to abolish the Roman-Dutch law and make the English law applicable to South Africa, said that the objections to divorce on the ground of desertion arose only on the part of those who objected to divorce altogether because of the " alleged sacramental nature of the bond." " Even if cases of collusion were more frequent than they are," he added, " the evils would be less than those arising under a system which compels a husband and wife to maintain a purely nominal union with one who had deserted and broken the most essential part of the contract upon which the marriage union is founded." The same learned judge in one of his judgments said that the distinction between the adultery of the husband and that of the wife had no legal or moral ground, and that there was certainly no such distinction in the Roman-Dutch law.*

This survey of divorce in the British Empire may be concluded by saying that in British India, Burma and Zanzibar, the laws of the various native religious sects, which, like the law of China, have always allowed divorce by mutual consent, are recognised by Great Britain and administered in the courts established by her. It may not be inconvenient to add here that Japan, the present ally of Great Britain, was

* *Journal of the Society of Comparative Legislation,* June, 1901.

admitted to the family of civilised nations in 1890, and her Civil Code of that year was compiled after a careful examination of the various laws in force in Western Civilisation, and " with the collaboration of European and American jurists." By that Code divorce by mutual consent is recognised without any inquiry into the causes of divorce, the parties simply going through the process of un-marrying before a public official. Where the parties do not consent, divorce is allowed upon such grounds as adultery, certain crimes, cruelty or grave insult rendering the common life intolerable, and desertion.*

The various systems of divorce in force in the British Empire, though of an " infinite variety," are only a microcosm on a large scale of the extraordinary diversity of the laws of divorce which exists in the rest of the civilised world. The will of the people, wherever it has had a voice in legislation, though slow-moving, and though it has had to face the traditional obstacles which England has placed in its way wherever amendments have been proposed, has, as has been seen, effected considerable reforms, though these reforms, owing to the same influence, have been hedged round by arbitrary restrictions which

* Burge, 2nd ed., I, p. 40 ; III, pp. 902-903 ; *Law Quarterly Review*, Jan., 1907, p. 42 ; art. by Munroe Smith.

have been concessions to the dogma of the indissolubility of marriage, while England herself has stood still in the matter. It has been seen that, by one of the ironies of history, one of the greatest of Protestant nations has been mainly instrumental in perpetuating and spreading all over the world the Catholic Canon law made by the monks of the Middle Ages.

XII

THE PRESENT POSITION AND TENDENCIES

"No serious historical work is worth the writing or the reading unless it conveys a moral, but to be useful the moral must develop itself in the mind of the reader without being obtruded upon him. Especially is this the case in a history treating of a subject which has called forth the fiercest passions of man, arousing alternately his highest and his basest impulses. I have not paused to moralise, but I have missed my aim if the events narrated are not so presented as to teach their appropriate lesson."

H. C. LEA, "A History of the Inquisition."

T HESE words of the historian of the Inquisition may be applied to the story which has been told in the preceding pages, in which the spirit of the Inquisition has been seen to be one of the most prominent influences. The stream of divorce has now been traced from its source through its main tributaries down to the troubled waters of our own time. While the reader may be left to draw his own moral from the facts which have been narrated, it remains to summarise briefly what mankind has gained and lost during the twenty centuries which have been under review, to indicate what are the principles and tendencies of legislation which history has established, and to sum up as shortly as possible the modern position.

The divorce laws, as we have seen, did not fall from Heaven like manna, but were established, as all other laws have been established, in the clash of conflicting interests, the warring of the creeds, and the stress of political expediency. They commenced in Europe with the ancient customs of the Roman, Germanic and Frankish peoples, who by a slow process of evolution had come to regard marriage as the most intimate, the most important and the most venerable of all partnerships, in which husband and wife were equal partners. Being based upon consent and affection alone, that partnership could be dissolved by the dissent of the parties when affection had turned into aversion, without the necessity of having to disclose the secret causes of their dissension, and without having to prosecute each other before a public tribunal. This law remained the practice of Europe, and had the sanction of the Christian Emperors of Rome until the beginning of the Middle Ages, when the Churches, obtaining temporal power, began to replace it by laws based upon interpretations of the well-known Scriptural texts. In the East of Europe the Eastern Church, though declaring marriage to be a sacrament, did not declare it to be indissoluble, but while retaining the elements of dogma which had been incorporated into the Roman law by the Christian Emperors, established the practice that divorce could only be obtained from an ecclesiastical tribunal on any of the grounds of the Roman law except mutual consent. This practice has been considerably modified by the lapse of time, but still remains in its essential principles in the Eastern countries of Europe, except that marriage has been declared to be a civil contract and divorce is now regulated by the State through its legislative and judicial machinery. Other grounds for divorce have been added which are more in agreement with the practice of Western Europe, the rights of husband and wife have been to a great extent equalised, while in Roumania divorce by mutual consent has been restored. Traces of an ecclesiastical law which preferred celibacy to marriage and the rights of the husband to those of the wife still remain in all these countries. Judicial separation as a substitute for divorce, however, was never adopted by the Eastern Church or the Eastern States of Europe.

In the West the Canon law was made under

similar influences to those in the East, and the Catholic Church, having declared marriage to be indissoluble, proceeded to establish the practice of dissolving it, but only in the publicity of an ecclesiastical tribunal, and only where one of the parties was guilty of some criminal or immoral act, of which adultery was the principal one. Though divorce was granted extensively, one or both of the parties were frequently condemned to either temporary or permanent celibacy and other forms of punishment, and judicial separation in lieu of divorce was invented. This conception of divorce was established by the Church, acting in conjunction with absolute rulers, while the wishes, welfare and affection of the parties were ignored. By this law the wife was placed in a condition of almost indissoluble subjection to her husband. The Canon law was denounced and resisted from the first by the people, and in the sixteenth century was abolished by the Reformation, which re-iterated the secular and contractual nature of marriage. The Reformers, however, after they had repressed the people, made a new law of divorce, re-established the Canon law which they had condemned as anti-Christian, and added to the grounds for divorce another crime, newly invented by them and said to be based upon the

Scriptures, which they called "malicious" desertion. The practice of the old episcopal courts was continued under the new *régime* in some countries by secular tribunals, and, while all the restrictions of the Canon law were adopted, the guilty party had to suffer added drastic penalties. Gradually these penalties disappeared, and the laws made by the Reformers were extended by judicial interpretation to include divorce on the ground of certain diseases and other crimes, till they become more in conformity with the welfare of the parties, though their wishes were still ignored, and where both parties desired divorce and assisted each other in obtaining it, this was treated as collusion or fraud, as it had been under the Canon law, and divorce was refused to both. The Canon law and the laws made by the Reformers still remain in force in many countries of Europe and in the colonies and states descended from them, though the rigour of these laws has been in many respects mitigated.

From the time of the Roman Emperors, however, it was seen by eminent thinkers and legislators, who were actuated by a desire for the liberty and welfare of the people, that it was impossible to attempt to base a human law of divorce upon any of the conflicting interpretations of the Scriptural texts, and at length by the French Revolution the Roman law of divorce, which had long been recognised by some as not being in conflict with the spirit of Christianity, was taken as the basis of legislation. The contractual nature of marriage was again affirmed, and divorce by mutual consent or at the will of either party without the necessity of any inquiry into the causes of the divorce was re-established. Divorce by mutual consent, which had always remained in force in Switzer- land, remained the law of Germany from the time of the French Revolution until a decade ago, and is still recognised in Austria, Belgium, Roumania, Norway, Portugal, Japan and apparently in Mexico.* In Germany, Denmark, Sweden and some of the American States, though a judicial inquiry into the causes of divorce is still required, divorce is allowed where it is recognised that the parties are irreconcilable, even though no so-called Scriptural ground or criminal offence is proved. Thus the tendency of legislation since the French Revolution, caused largely by its influence, is to make divorce depend upon the wishes and welfare of the parties as in the Roman law and ancient customs of Europe, while the impossibility of basing the law of divorce upon irrecon-

* Loewy, *The Civil Code of the German Empire*, note on art. 1564.

cilable texts of the Scriptures has been almost universally recognised. Marriage is now by the law of every country of the world treated as a civil contract. Though these principles have been established only after a long struggle for liberty, and there have been reactions caused by the attempt on the part of some dominant caste, religious or secular, to recover its lost power and privileges, they may be said to represent the will of the people, wherever it has had an opportunity of declaring itself, and the decision of the most eminent thinkers and legislators of different creeds and philosophies who have preferred the liberty and welfare of the people to any particular form of dogma. The present chaos of the divorce laws by which what is condemned as immoral in some countries is regarded as moral and desirable in others, and which compels many to discard their nationality or domicil in order to obtain a divorce which is forbidden to them in their own country, is solely the result of the application of laws derived from Scriptural texts and of the consequent conflict between liberty and dogma. The only solution appears to lie, not in any attempt to harmonise the conflicting interpretations of conflicting passages of Scripture, but to return to the simple principles of the Roman law.

A HISTORY OF DIVORCE

Although, as we have seen, the dogma of the indissolubility of marriage has never been practised at any time, not even when the Church had the best opportunity of enforcing it, some form of that dogma has always been a strong vested or reactionary interest in legislation, which has succeeded in many countries in introducing certain arbitrary compromises and restrictions which are neither in conformity with the wishes and welfare of the parties nor with any accepted interpretation of the Scriptures. Thus in some countries an arbitrary period of delay varying from one to ten years has been fixed as being necessary before divorce can be granted on the ground of desertion. Similarly, in the Roman-Dutch law, the fiction of an order for the restitution of conjugal rights, which the Courts cannot enforce, is a necessary condition precedent to an action for divorce on the ground of desertion. One of the most striking compromises was that of the adoption of judicial separation by the Reformers to cover cases in which the parties found it impossible or impracticable to live together owing to causes which were often graver than adultery or desertion, such as an attempt upon each other's lives. Judicial separation is still retained in most systems, either as the only remedy open to the parties where they consent, or as an alternative remedy which at the request of either party may be converted into a divorce. In the Code Napoléon a similar compromise was arrived at in order to conciliate the Catholic Church and the conservative lawyers, and divorce by mutual consent was hedged round with conditions which treated the parties as children requiring the consent of their parents. In the Austrian Code the compromise has taken the form of allowing divorce by mutual consent to non-Catholics, while Catholics, even though they renounce their creed, are only allowed the remedy of judicial separation. In Russia a similar compromise has been noticed. Such compromises, however, are all based upon the obsolete principle of legislating for particular creeds or in accordance with the wishes of an established church or a dominant religious sect. While it is difficult to understand why Catholics who believe in the indissolubility of marriage should require judicial separation, it is manifestly unjust that they should legally be deprived of the remedy of divorce if they desire it, while it is even more unjust that they should compel others of different creeds to be obliged to resort to a remedy which condemns both parties to celibacy. The most recent legislation upon the

261

subject of divorce, that of Norway, is based upon the only practicable principle of legislation in modern life. There divorce, either by mutual consent or upon grounds which establish the impossibility of matrimonial harmony, is allowed to all, and should the parties desire a judicial separation they are at liberty to obtain it. In that country divorce is treated, as we have seen, not as a crime but as a misfortune, and the immorality of the retention of a purely nominal tie against the wishes of the parties is fully recognised.

Legislation in these matters, however, moves slowly, and survivals of obsolete ecclesiastical laws still remain in the systems of many countries. It has been seen that the modern trial of divorce cases was the invention of monks in the Middle Ages for their own ends, and that the modern judge with his wide discretion to refuse, and in some countries to allow divorce, is the direct legal descendant of the ecclesiastical officials who presided over the episcopal courts, the Inquisition and the confessional, and his function has even been said to be that of a deity. While it can never be to the public interest that the secrets of unfortunate spouses should be disclosed in a public court, even if any court is justified or competent to judge between the parties, the trial of such causes in a more private manner is at best a mere palliative, substituting the confessional for the Inquisition. That consent between the parties must necessarily mean collusion or fraud could only emanate, as it did emanate, from the minds of mediæval monks, who treated the parties, as they are treated in modern law, as children. The idea that divorce can only be obtained on the ground of some crime and that divorce in itself is a sort of crime arises from the same origin. The trial of divorce remains in many modern countries a matter of " public violence," as it was described by one of the Reformation lawyers, and the parties are expected to publicly establish their own innocence or guilt, and, in order to obtain the exclusive custody of the children—which is rarely if ever granted—or certain proprietary advantages, they are encouraged to make every attempt to blacken each other's characters to the delectation of a callous public. Public opinion, when it condemns both parties irrespective of their guilt or innocence, is merely exercising the right of excommunication which was once taught as the duty of the faithful at a time when the Catholic Church had the monopoly over divorce. This modern excommunication has been well described by William

Morris as a "hypocritical excommunication which people are *forced* to pronounce, either by unconsidered habit or by the unexpressed threat of the lesser interdict if they are lax in their hypocrisy." But while crime is often the only ground sufficient to entitle either party to a divorce, where that crime is doubled it is insufficient for divorce in many countries, though some countries, such as Germany, have abolished this anomaly. In many countries divorce can be obtained only if the innocent party chooses to sue for a divorce, and where he chooses to perpetuate a nominal tie and to condemn the other party to perpetual celibacy or immorality, the other party has no remedy, and public opinion endorses the inaction of the innocent spouse, who may be guilty of worse offences of which the law takes no cognisance. Marriage indeed, as Mr. Lecky says, "gives either party an extraordinary power of injuring the other." *

The question of divorce in England has always been closely connected with the privileges of the clergy of the Established Church. Before finally parting from the question of the indissolubility

---

* As a writer in the *North American Review* (July, 1906, p. 70), says, the effect of such a law is "the condemnation of many to practical celibacy or sexual outlawry."

of marriage it may be useful to refer to a modern English exponent of that doctrine who advocates it not only as a religious tenet but as a principle of legislation. It has been seen that it was only by a series of historical accidents that the views of More, Cranmer, Milton and Gladstone did not become the law of England, and it is a subject for profitable speculation to consider what many who now oppose all divorce reform in England would have thought if the views of these representatives of different creeds had been established as legal tradition. The present Bishop of Oxford, in a recent book, advocates the absolute indissolubility of marriage, and does not disguise his desire to have it made the law of the land. The learned author effectively acknowledges the impossibility of basing a law of divorce upon the Scriptural texts when he tells us that fifteen years ago he accepted the interpretation of St. Matthew which allowed divorce, but that now he is a follower of other apostles who, according to his revision of the Scriptures, deny the right of divorce altogether. The historical aspect of the question has already been sufficiently treated in the foregoing pages, and it is far from my ambition to attempt to settle a theological problem which St. Augustine confessed his inability to solve. Whatever be the theological solution—a matter which solely concerns the individual conscience, and should not, as Mr. Gladstone said, be allowed to influence legislation—it is clear that St. Paul allowed divorce in certain cases which have been variously interpreted to mean religious differences, heresy, and malicious desertion. It is also clear that St. John, who stated what he considered to be the essential doctrines of Christianity, is entirely silent upon the subject of divorce. As all attempts to follow the conflicting interpretations of other apostles have utterly failed in legislation, it may be that the truth of the matter is to be found in the silence of St. John. As to the spirit of Christianity, the liberal views of thinkers from Grotius to Gladstone have been sufficiently indicated, but it may safely be said that that spirit is contrary to compelling persons to remain in a state of hypocrisy to themselves and to the world against their wills, where there can be no injury to any one by a divorce. Divorce by mutual consent or where neither of the parties suffers by it appears to be nowhere condemned or even dealt with in the Scriptures, which also nowhere lay down the necessity of a public or any other trial for divorce. A reference to the ideal marriage, which, of course, is indissoluble

—for as the Emperor Leo said : "Who would wish to separate himself from an ideal partner ?" —was as necessary then as it is now, when harsh treatment of wives by husbands and attempts by the latter to justify themselves by the law and the Scriptures are not altogether unknown. But whatever the words of the well-known Scriptural texts may mean, there appears to be considerable doubt as to whether the words themselves have been accurately reported, conflicting as they are in many important respects. The Rev. W. Hobhouse, in his Bampton Lectures, says : "Assuming that the Gospels, Acts and Epistles are genuine documents, can we be sure that they give a true and accurate account of our Lord's teaching ? . . . It is round this question . . . that the battle of criticism will rage in the immediate future." But humanity has definitely refused to depend for its laws upon the battles of dogmatists, and only wishes to have a reasonable law of divorce to meet the exigencies which unfortunately arise, and have always arisen, even where marriage was in legal theory indissoluble. Bishop Gore admits that the doctrine which he advocates is "one of the precepts of Christianity most difficult to flesh and blood," and that modern people are "unable to accept it." But as the opinions of men are in a state of uncertainty, he urges us to " throw all our influence as citizens in resisting any proposal to relax the existing allowance of divorce by the State." The injustice which women suffer under that law he does not even notice, while the position of the poor under it he dismisses as unimportant. No Englishman has ever advocated the doctrine of indissolubility as an individual religious belief with greater force than the late Mr. Gladstone, and the reader may be left to judge between the statesmanship of Mr. Gladstone on the one hand, and the whole bench of bishops in 1857 and the present Bishop of Oxford on the other.*

It has been seen that from the time when ecclesiastics first laid down the laws of divorce the rights of married women have been subordinated to those of their husbands, and that it is only in comparatively recent times that they have been restored to a position of comparative equality. Women have been taught the duty of matrimonial subordination for centuries, but there is every indication that they are beginning to insist upon their rights to be treated as independent persons, " irrespective

* Gore, *The Question of Divorce* ; W. Hobhouse, *The Church and the World.*

of sex, even if special relations and conditions are willingly incurred under the form of partnership involved in marriage." Women are beginning to see that the present divorce laws, conflicting as they are, were not written by the unalterable hand of destiny, but were made by men, and principally by monks, for their own ends. It has been seen that, from the first, attempts have been made by a few solitary thinkers to protect those who had no means of protecting themselves, and to place in the hands of married women, in the right of divorce, " a sheathed sword " which they might use in case of necessity. The stigma which monks and ecclesiastics at all times have succeeded in attaching to divorce for any cause whatever has always resulted in women condemning divorced women in all cases even more bitterly than men. By all the survivals of dogmatism which have been already noticed it is invariably the woman who suffers more than the man, and the paramount right which the husband has always, according to these laws, been allowed to exercise over the children whom she has borne, has, more than any other cause, compelled many women to continue, in outward appearance at least, in the degradation of a marriage with husbands for whom they have long ceased to have any affection.

In the matter of domicil, as we have seen, the woman's rights are entirely subordinated to those of the man, although the modern tendency is to grant to the wife in all respects a separate domicil. While little has been done by their masters to alleviate their lot in a matter which concerns them much more intimately than men, the recent law of Norway establishes the perfect legal equality of husband and wife and the right of a married woman after divorce, except in certain cases, to maintenance by her husband until she marries again or is in a position to maintain herself; such a provision being necessary in modern economic conditions by which the wife in many, but not in all, cases during marriage is incapacitated from earning her own living, while by her domestic duties she assists her husband in earning the common property. It is worthy of notice that modern Socialists, as part of their programme of social reform, strongly advocate a more liberal divorce law and the absolute equality of husband and wife. The abolition of all judicial inquiry into the causes of the differences between the parties, their right to dissolve the contract either by mutual consent or at the finally expressed will of either party, and the registration of divorce by a public court or official, are essential parts of modern Socialism. Many who have found that reforms in these vitally important matters are not generally to be obtained by the aid of any of the traditional political or ecclesisatical organisations are undoubtedly beginning to turn their attention to Socialism.*

It has been frequently noticed by historians that supporters of some form of dogma, when they find that the indissolubility of marriage is untenable as a practical proposal, set up objections to divorce on various pretexts, such as the danger to the stability of the family and to the interests of morality and of the children, and even contend that the public trial of divorce acts as a deterrent. These various objections to divorce, which would be applicable, if they have any cogency, to all laws of divorce, have already been considered in the course of this book, and it would be foreign to its purpose to deal with them in detail. The argument that the public trial of divorce acts as a deterrent—which it undoubtedly does in the case of women—is only of any value if divorce is a crime, and the argument is only used because divorce has so

---

* A. Stoddart, *The New Socialism* ; Annette M. B. Meakin, *Woman in Transition* ; W. Morris, *News from Nowhere* (5th ed.), pp. 61-64 ; G. B. Shaw, *Getting Married*, preface thereto and pp. 167 and foll. ; *Encyclopædia Britannica* (11th ed.), Art. "Woman" ; Lichtenberger, *Divorce*, pp. 187-8, 197.

long been associated with crime. The difficulties which are placed in the way of divorce
as a rule punish the innocent more than the
guilty, for while the fear of public scandal en-
genders the practice of Machiavellian arts,
where there is no marriage in reality there are
many who, cognisant of the inherent injustice of
the laws, are not deterred by them from committing the only so-called crime or crimes which
the law recognises as grounds for dissolving
marriage, while those who scorn to make use of
these methods and wish to retain the approval
of their fellow-men, suffer most of all by the
present laws. The influence of liberal laws of
divorce upon morality and the stability of the
family, according to the practice of many
countries, has always been a salutary one, and
the connection between divorce and immorality
has been seen to be at most problematical. None
of these objections to divorce have been considered sufficient by those statesmen who have
advocated more liberal laws, and who have had
the integrity and morality of marriage at heart.
The verdict of history appears to be that where
marriage is indissoluble or has only been allowed
for some crime, morality has suffered, while where
death or crime alone dissolves marriage, death,
being wished for, has often been accelerated

and crime committed. If one of two incompatible spouses, unable to obtain a divorce, relieves the other by dying naturally, that other is allowed by both law and public opinion to marry one with whom a union in the lifetime of both would have been condemned as guilty. The interests of the children did not prevent Justinian from imprisoning the parents in monasteries or the Popes from separating them, often for ever. These considerations, as we have seen, played no part when the laws were made, at a time when the wishes and welfare of parents and children were equally ignored so long as the parents outwardly conformed to whatever dogma happened to be in fashion. Objections on the ground of utility are therefore open to the suspicion that utility is not the real intention of those who propose them. As Mr. Lecky says, the burden of proof is on those who say that marriage is not dissoluble by the parties like any other contract. "Of all contracts, it is that which is most frequently entered into under the influence of blinding passion and at an age when experience and knowledge of life are immature, and it is a contract in which happiness and misery mainly depend upon conditions of character and temper that are often most imperfectly disclosed. It is the most intimate of

273

all relations . . . it may, if it fails in its purpose, become in the highest degree calamitous, and it gives either party an extraordinary power of injuring the other." Before questions of utility can be considered, the rights of the parties, which they had before dogma began to operate upon the law, should first be restored, according to the well-known principle of the Canon law— *Spoliatus ante omnia restituendus.**

The law of divorce has been seen to have commenced in the customs established by the people, and afterwards the will of a few who preferred dogma to utility displaced those customs by a different law until at length the people, who are now the sole source of political power, have tended to restore ancient liberty. Though dogma has been discarded as a source of legislation, it has played and still plays so important a part in forming or influencing public opinion, especially as it is supported by many of the official exponents of various creeds, that the future of divorce reform is uncertain. The undoubted indifference of many who hope that that will never be obliged to make use of the remedy of divorce is one of the elements which

* J. Bryce, *Studies in History and Jurisprudence*, II, p. 467 ; W. E. H. Lecky, *Democracy and Liberty*, II, p. 158, and *History of European Morals*, II, ch. V, p. 353.

strengthens that uncertainty, and makes reaction in the future as possible and reform as fluctuating as it has been in the past. As Milton says: " When points of difficulty are to be discussed appertaining to the removal of unreasonable wrong and burden from the perplexed life of our brother, it is incredible how cold, how dull, and far from all fellow-feeling we are without the spur of self-concernment." While the criminal laws have been in many important respects shorn of their mediæval barbarism, many who are only too ready to " cast the first stone " at any one who is so unhappy in his or her married life that they have sought the remedy to which the law entitles them, whether or not they be guilty of what the law no longer regards as a crime, will always be ready to sign a petition for the reprieve of the lowest criminal. The task of the modern reformer is made all the more difficult when it is remembered that it is only through the instrumentality of public opinion, composed as it is of different elements and interests, or in its name, that any reform can be made.

Such is the price which modern civilisation has to pay for what are now universally acknowledged by historians to have been the errors of the monks of the Dark Ages. The belief in witchcraft and demons and the punishment of heresy have long since disappeared, but the spirit of the Inquisition and the maxims of Machiavelli which accompanied the divorce laws of the Middle Ages, still survive in the modern laws and opinions about divorce. "The judgment of impartial history," says Mr. Lea, "must be that the Inquisition was the monstrous offspring of mistaken zeal," a statement which is applicable to the laws of divorce which were forced upon humanity in the same dark period of human history. Of the facts which have been narrated in the course of this history there can be no dispute, and of the opinions which have been expressed in the present chapter, which are the opinions of "many zealous friends of human progress," the reader may be left to judge from those facts, the present writer "being fully of opinion," in the words of Sir William Blackstone, "that if his principles be false and his doctrines unwarrantable, no apology from himself can make them right; if founded in truth and rectitude, no censure from others can make them wrong."

AUTHORITIES AND REFERENCES

ABRAHAMS, I. Jewish Life in the Middle Ages (1896).

ACTON, LORD. History of Freedom, and other essays (1907).

AMSTERDAM, STADBOEK VAN.

ANCIENT LAWS AND INSTITUTES OF ENGLAND, printed by command of H.M. William IV., under the direction of the Commissioners on the Public Records of the Kingdom, and containing the laws of Ethelbert and Canute and the *Liber Pœnitentialis* of Theodore, Archbishop of Canterbury (1840).

ANDREAE, S. J. FOCKEMA. Annotationes ad Grotium.

AN EXPOSITION OF CERTAINE DIFFICULT AND OBSCURE WORDS AND TERMES OF THE LAWES OF THIS REALME IN ENGLISH AND FRENCH (London 1609).

ARNTZENIUS, H. J. Institutiones Juris Belgici Civilis.

BANCROFT, G. History of the United States.

BENTHAM, J. Theory of Legislation.

BIGG, C. Origins of Christianity.

BISHOP, J. P. Marriage and Divorce (1873).

BLACKSTONE, SIR W. Commentaries on the Laws of England (15th ed.).

BLOK, P. J.   History of the Netherlands (tr. by O. Bierstadt and R. Putnam, 1898, etc.).

BOURINOT, Sir J. G.   Parliamentary Procedure and Practice in Canada (3rd ed., 1903).

BOUVIER'S LAW DICTIONARY, U.S. ed. Rawle.

BROUWER, H.   De Jure Connubiorum (2nd ed., 1714).

BROWNE, G.   Law and Practice in Divorce and Matrimonial Causes (4th ed., 1880).

BRYCE, J.   Studies in History and Jurisprudence (1901).

BURGE, W.   Commentaries on Colonial and Foreign Laws ; 1st ed., 1838 ; 2nd ed., 1907-1910, vols. 1-3.

BURN, D. R.   Ecclesiastical Law (1824).

BURNET, BISHOP.   History of the Reformation (1865).
History of His Own Time (1818, 1865, and ed. O. Airy, 1897, etc.).

BYNKERSHOEK, C. van. Quaestiones Juris Privati.

CALVIN, J.   Lexicon Magnum (Geneva, 1683).

CAMBRIDGE MODERN HISTORY.   12 vols.

CANONES SANCTORUM ET VENERENDORUM APOS-TOLORUM (CORPUS JURIS CIVILIS, AM-STERDAM, 1700, vol II.).

CLARK, C.   Summary of Colonial Law (1834).

CLIFFORD, F.   History of Private Bill Legislation.   2 vols.   (1885 and 1887).

COCCEJI, S. VON. Jus Civile Controversum (1740).

CODE CIVIL (Code Napoléon), ed. 1825.

AUTHORITIES AND REFERENCES

CONNECTICUT. Special Acts and Resolutions (vol. 14).

CORPUS JURIS CANONICI (P. Lancellotti, 1682).

CORPUS JURIS CIVILIS (ed. 1700, Amsterdam).

DANTE, ALIGHIERI. Inferno, Purgatorio and Paradiso.

DICEY, A. V. Law of the Constitution, 3rd. ed. (1889).

ENCYCLOPÆDIA BRITANNICA, 11th ed.

ERASMUS, D. Colloquia (1719 ed.).

FROUDE, A. Divorce of Catherine of Aragon (1893).
Life and Letters of Erasmus (1906).

FRUIN, J. A. Nederlandsche Wetboeken (Dutch Codes), 1896.

GEMMILL, J. A. The Practice of the Parliament of Canada upon Bills of Divorce (1889).

GIBBON, E. Decline and Fall of the Roman Empire.

GRAHAM, H. A Group of Scottish Women.

GRATIAN. Decretum.

GREGORY IX. Decretales.

GROENEWEGEN. De Legibus Abrogatis.

GROTIUS. Introduction to Dutch Jurisprudence (tr. Maasdorp).
Rights of Peace and War, with notes by Barbeyrac (London, 1738).

HALLAM, H. Constitutional History of England, 7th ed. (1854).

HANSARD'S PARLIAMENTARY DEBATES.

281

HARNACK, A. History of Dogma (tr. J. Millar).

HEINECCIUS. Antiquitatum Romanorum (3rd ed., 1730).

HIRSH, H. Tabulated Digest of the Divorce Laws of the United States (1901).

HOBHOUSE, L. T. Morals in Evolution.

HOBHOUSE, W. The Church and the World (Bampton Lectures, 1st ed.).

HOLDSWORTH, W. S. A History of English Law (1909).

HOLLANDSCHE CONSULTATIEN EN ADVIJSEN (Rotterdam, 5de deel 1689).

HOWARD, G. E. A History of Matrimonial Institutions. 3 vols. (1904).

JEWISH ENCYCLOPÆDIA, *s.v.* Divorce.

JOURNAL OF THE SOCIETY OF COMPARATIVE LEGISLATION (New Series).

KENT, J. Commentaries on American Law.

KOSTLIN, J. Life of Luther (Eng. tr., 1900).

LAW QUARTERLY REVIEW, vol. i., p. 355 (1885) ; vol. xx., no. 80, p. 363, Oct., 1904 ; Jan., 1907, p. 42.

LEA, H. C. Sacerdotal Celibacy (1867).
Studies in Church History (1869).
A History of the Inquisition (1888).

LECKY, W. E. H. Democracy and Liberty (1896).
History of European Morals (1902).
History of Rationalism (1900).

AUTHORITIES AND REFERENCES

LEI DO DIVORCIO (decree of 3 Nov., 1910, of Portugal).

LEYSER, A. à. Meditationes ad Pandectas (1772).

LICHTENBERGER, J. P. Divorce: A Study in Social Causation (1909).

LODGE. History of Modern Europe.

LOEWY, W. The Civil Code of the German Empire (translated, 1909).

MACHIAVELLI. The Prince.

MACQUEEN, J. Jurisdiction of the House of Lords (1842).

MEAKIN, ANNETTE M. B. Woman in Transition.

MILL, J. S. Autobiography.
Letters (1910).
Subjection of Women.
On Liberty.

MILTON. The Doctrine and Discipline of Divorce.

MONTESQUIEU. The Spirit of the Laws. (Translation by Mrs. Nugent, 1752).

MORE, SIR T. Utopia.

MORRIS, W. News from Nowhere (1897).

MUIRHEAD. History of Roman Law (2nd ed., Goudy).

MUNSTERBERG, H., Prof. The Americans. (Translated by E. B. Holt, 1905).

NINETEENTH CENTURY AND AFTER, No. 420 (Feb., 1912), p. 364, article by J. Castberg.

PERKINS, A. Life of Mrs. Norton.

POLLOCK AND MAITLAND. History of English Law.

POTHIER. Pandectae (1818 ed., Paris).

Traité du Contrat de Mariage (2 vols., ed. Paillet, 1813, in Œuvres).

PUFENDORF. Le Droit de la Nature et des Gens (ed. 1759, with notes by Barbeyrac).

Law of Nature and of Nations, tr. by B. Kennett (Oxford, 1710).

QUARTERLY REVIEW. Oct., 1911.

REPORTS ON THE LAWS OF MARRIAGE AND DIVORCE IN FOREIGN COUNTRIES (1894 and 1903, Parliamentary Papers).

RITTERSHUSIUS, C. Differentiarum Juris Civilis and Canonici (ed. 1668).

ROGER, A. and SOREL, A. Codes et Lois Usuelles (Paris, 1897).

SELDEN, J.

Table Talk.

Uxor Ebraica (Works, 1726).

SHAW, G. B. Getting Married.

SOUTH AFRICA. Reports of the Supreme Court of Cape Colony, Transvaal and Eastern Districts Court.

SPANHEMIUS, F. Dubia Evangelia (ed. 1700, Geneva).

ST. AUGUSTINE. Confessions.

STANLEY, Dean. Lectures on the Eastern Church.

AUTHORITIES AND REFERENCES

STATUTES of the United Kingdom, of the Colonies, and of the United States of America.

STODDART, A. M.   The New Socialism.

STOKES, A.   A View of the Constitution of the British Colonies in N. America and the West Indies (1793).

STRYPE, J.   Memorials of Cranmer.

TILSCH, E.   Article on Austrian Divorce, in *Journal of the Society of Comparative Legislation*, vol. xxv., July, 1911.

UNITED STATES, The Federal and State Constitutions, Colonial Charters and Organic Laws of (1878).

VAN DER KEESSEL.   Select Theses.

VAN DER LINDEN.   Institutes.

VAN LEEUWEN.   Censura Forensis.

VAN ZYL, C. H.   Judicial Practice of South Africa (2nd ed.).

VOET, J.   Commentarius ad Pandectas.

VOORDA, B.   Theses (1773).

VOORDA, J.   Interpretationes et Emendationes (1735, Utrecht).

WESSELS, Sir J.   History of the Roman-Dutch Law (1908).

WETBOEK NAPOLEON (proclaimed by Louis Napoleon King of Holland, 1809).

WHEELER, G. J.   Confederation Law of Canada (1896).

ZURCK.   Codex Batavus (1711).

INDEX

INDEX

INDEX

INDEX

INDEX

INDEX

292

INDEX

293

CPSIA information can be obtained
at www.ICGtesting.com
Printed in the USA
BVHW011915060422
633607BV00002B/9